SHAPING CHARACTER

SHAPING
CHARACTER

Moral Education in the Christian College

Arthur F. Holmes

William B. Eerdmans Publishing Company
Grand Rapids, Michigan

Library of Congress Cataloging-in-Publication Data

Holmes, Arthur Frank, 1924-
Shaping character: moral education in the Christian college /
Arthur F. Holmes.
p.   cm.
Includes bibliographical references (p.   ) and index.
ISBN 0-8028-0497-7
1. Moral education—United States.   2. Education, Higher—United States.
I. Title.
LC311.H57   1991
378'.014'0973—dc20   90-47019
                                                                    CIP

Contents

Contents

Preface

Education has to do with the transmission of values, whether it be the value of learning, the value of scientific knowledge, so-called "American" values, aesthetic values, or moral values. Higher education in America is rightly concerned with student values. And within the whole range of values education the Christian college has long regarded moral education as central to its mandate.

In the nineteenth century the capstone in a college curriculum was a moral philosophy course taught by the college president to integrate the student's education and shape the conscience in regards to economic, political, and social affairs. The emergence of separate social sciences in these areas changed all that, for they were to be empirical, value-free studies. Ethics gradually became an isolated subspeciality in the philosophy or religion department, an elective on a par with many others. Yet even then moral education remained a distinctive concern: religion courses were still required, chapel talks extolled the virtues, in loco parentis rules set behavioral limitations, and concerned administrators and professors still tended to moralize.

Today Christian colleges claim as their distinctive concern

an active integration of faith and learning across the entire curriculum, and the penetration of a Christian worldview into all of life and learning. As one aspect of this integrative task, and with the support of the Pew Charitable Trust, the Christian College Consortium and its thirteen member colleges in 1986 launched an "Ethics Across the Curriculum" project involving both faculty and curriculum development. The aim was to extend and strengthen ethics teaching in general education and in every major offered. As coordinator of this project I was forced to read and think and learn and speak extensively about ethics and the teaching of ethics. To round out my involvement, it therefore seemed appropriate to draw together some of the ideas and information and sense of direction that emerged, and to offer it for whatever use it may have to faculty and administrators and students as a stimulus and catalyst for their own thinking and practical guidance.

In effect, "Ethics Across the Curriculum" represented a return to the vision behind that moral philosophy course of over a century ago, that every student should be systematically exposed to ethical dimensions of life and learning. For the scene has changed: while the social sciences no longer claim the positivist objectivity and value-free stance of the past, work in applied ethics has burgeoned in many fields, normative ethical theory is again an active and exciting discipline, and promising new insights about character and the role of community have emerged in Christian ethics. Meanwhile, moral-development theory has made significant strides. In all these regards the time is ripe for concerted efforts at moral education and character formation in the Christian college.

Ethics is far too important and ethical issues far too pervasive to be left just to the specialist. This little book is addressed to the nonspecialist, the student, the science or literature or history or business professor, the nonethicist administrator or teacher. In a word this book is for the intelligent amateur who is trying to understand moral education and find her or his place in it. It is a survey, an introduction, and, rather than trying to cover all the literature and all the issues, it concentrates on distinctively Christian concerns both in the objectives it proposes and in the questions it raises about moral development theory and moral education in general. For those wanting a more in-depth treatment, a variety of resources are already available, some of which are noted in a concluding bibliography.

Not much of this book is particularly original except for the eleven objectives introduced in the first chapter, the overall framework to which they give rise, and the focus on Christian perspectives. My debts therefore are great. Robert C. Roberts critiqued my discussion of values and virtues, and Richard E. Butman shared with me the results to date of a current study of student values and decision making in three Christian colleges. Zondra Lindblade and Jon Sweeney offered helpful suggestions on the entire manuscript. In addition I must thank people on many campuses for their enthusiasm, their stimulating questions, criticisms, and insights, and for the opportunities they afforded me to try out some of these ideas. What other writers have contributed to my thinking will become evident along the way, but not what groups of faculty in seminars and workshops contributed. My hope is that they will be joined by many others in many other institutions across the country in addressing more informedly and systematically this task which is so central to Christian higher education and to education at large.

Chapter One

College Is for Character

Some years ago a professor in the fine arts approached me and hesitantly asked if a course in ethics was offered in our philosophy department or whether it would be somewhere else. Ethics was apparently a subject with which he had little acquaintance: he wasn't at all sure where it might fit in a college curriculum, or if there was such an academic subject at all.

That sounds like an extreme case, but where would a professional artist encounter ethics in the course of his specialized training? On the surface it might seem that music performance is value free—not aesthetically, of course, but as far as ethics is concerned. How different is it in that regard from statistical research or experimental physics? And if science and art seem value free, what do people in those fields have to do with ethics? Ethics is not their business.

Or is it? What about plagiarizing in music, about respecting an audience, about pride and excessive self-assertion? Are these not ethical concerns? Is musical artistry amoral?

The idea that education could be value free was quite alien to American higher education a hundred years ago, for the college was supposed to offer moral guidance, to inculcate wisdom, and to teach students to value truth, beauty, and goodness. Then came the positivist notion that learning could

1

be value free and a dominant cost-benefit approach to policy decisions. Historian J. H. Hexter likened it to "a professional prefrontal lobotomy that excises part of your intellectual capacity and all of your moral judgment"; it eliminates the pervasive value-bearing element from the very vocabulary historians use in writing about people. Addressing the American Historical Association, Hexter appealed to his colleagues to "abandon a position which we can sustain only at the cost of not saying what we know."[1]

In similar fashion Norman Lamm declares that value neutrality abandons the very premise on which the search for and transmission of knowledge is pursued—the superiority of education over ignorance, of reason over impulse, of discipline over slovenliness, of integrity as against cheating. He too calls for a return to the teaching of values in higher education.[2]

Yet even though value-free approaches have markedly declined, the aftermath continues to haunt us in the form of highly educated scientists, artists, and scholars who feel totally unprepared to address ethical issues related to their fields, or who find no time to address them in their courses, or even declare that ethics is not their business. The rise of postmodernism and the deconstructionist approach has only complicated the pervasive relativism of our times. For whatever reason, ethics has been either seriously neglected or seriously misconstrued.

Meantime, the growing pressure for career preparation in the 1970s threatened to squeeze both general education and values education. Earl McGrath, former U.S. secretary of education, argued for interweaving the three together.

> To discuss values outside of the context of general education would be to neglect the most perplexing educational issue of our day—how to assist the rank and file of students in reaching decisions on the complex political, social and moral problems which they will inevitably face. That instruction related to values

1. Quoted in *The Chronicle of Higher Education,* January 8, 1986, p. 10.
2. *New York Times,* October 14, 1986.

and career preparation must be interfused is all too manifest in the shocking gap which exists between the high occupational competence of many graduates and their low moral concern for the human consequences of their acts.[3]

In his inaugural address as president of New York University, John Sawhill struck a similar chord. After citing the relevance of history and philosophy to law, medicine, business, and administration, he continued:

> Doctors are now confronting moral decisions about the limits of sustaining life, and even about the definition of life itself. Lawyers and businessmen are being challenged to face up to complex ethical and moral controversies. Accountability for individual and institutional behavior is achieving renewed meaning in American life.[4]

Yet in 1986 the thirteen member colleges of the Christian College Consortium conducted self-studies to discover what was being done across the curriculum to teach ethics, in what departments and courses, by whom and with what preparation, materials, and methods. Apart from the occasional course and professor in religion or philosophy few claimed any competence or any preparation, and most departments admitted that little if anything was being done other than occasional moralizing or consciousness raising.

But the picture is changing. The activist 1960s awakened the social conscience of educators, evoking a tremendous surge of scholarly activity in applied ethics: business ethics, bio-ethics, environmental ethics, political ethics, professional ethics, computer ethics, sports ethics, research ethics, media ethics, and so forth. While philosophers are at the forefront of this movement it has also captured the energies and expertise of scholars and practitioners in many other fields. New journals have sprung

3. "Careers, Values and General Education," *Liberal Education* 60 (1974): 281.
4. Quoted in *N.Y.U. Alumni News*, January, 1976.

up, as well as a rash of textbooks, new scholarly organizations, ethics centers on university and college campuses, and courses in applied ethics in a wide variety of disciplines. Ethics is once again regarded as everybody's business. Ethics across the curriculum, while still not a reality, has become a realistic goal.

Why then should ethics be everybody's business? First, *it is an essential part of higher education to cultivate the qualities of a liberally educated person.* A liberal education is not job training, although it will of course have career outcomes. It is not just broad learning across various arts and sciences. Nor is it just an introduction to the heritage of our past: great events, great people, great ideas. Education helps shape people, cultivating abilities and qualities that last throughout life and transfer to a myriad of tasks.

These ideals for the liberally educated person include thinking ability, language and communication skills, decision making, social concern and responsibility, a sense of personal identity, and moral character. These should be overarching educational goals in history, music, physics, or theology, to help people think for themselves, communicate with empathy and precision and grace, make responsible decisions, and become the kinds of persons they are meant to be. In that sense ethics is everybody's business.

Second, as we have observed, *ethics should be a distinctive emphasis in Christian higher education.* The Christian college does not simply add biblical studies to a broader range of subjects, although even that could give Christian ethics a prominent place. Nor does the Christian college merely provide a pious and spiritually supportive environment for learning, although that too would mean ethics should be highlighted. The real distinctive is a holistic integration of faith and learning, an active penetration of all the disciplines and all life's callings with the beliefs and values that make up a Christian worldview. Ethics then belongs in all the disciplines: it *is* everybody's business.

Third, positivism notwithstanding, *values are intrinsic to the very subject matter we teach,* and these value dimensions cannot honestly be avoided. Values are ideals, good ends we ought to pursue. They are of various kinds: moral values like honesty, political values like equal justice for all, intellectual values like truth and understanding, aesthetic values like beauty, social values like friendship. All of life and learning comes value laden, laden with God-given possibilities for good. Those values I have just named are not arbitrarily imposed on things, but rather inhere in their respective aspects of life: thus one value intrinsic to intellectual activity is understanding, one intrinsic to art is beauty, one intrinsic to social relationships is friendship. These values are then objective, not relative to the individual or situation, rooted in universal aspects of our lives in God's creation. The various disciplines, in that they are human activities and their subject matter touches various aspects of God's creation, are therefore to some degree all value laden. The value of understanding and the value of scholarly honesty are the barest minimum, but ethical responsibility attends even these ideals. Ethics is again everybody's business.

Fourth, *values are inherent not only in what is taught but also in how it is taught.* My choice of teaching methods is loaded. By encouraging questions and challenges to my own interpretation of things I am teaching both honesty and the value of stretching our God-given minds. By the questions I pose to a student I facilitate the clarification and perhaps the improvement of her values. The Socratic method, modeled on dialog among friends, presupposes the worth of all participants and the values of friendship itself. In Plato's *Lysis,* dialog is the true art of lovers. How I teach, then, teaches an ethic. It models something good, bad, or both. What I am, what I choose to do, and how I do it are powerful influences on impressionable students, far more effective in many cases than ethical arguments or theoretical lectures on moral matters. For better or for worse, teaching ethics is what everybody already is doing.

But ethics is also everybody's business because it implies *a range of objectives* within which every teacher and student in every department—and every administrator and staff person,

5

for that matter—has a place. Later chapters will discuss these
objectives more fully and some of the teaching methods that can
be used, but for now consider these objectives that moral
education in a Christian context should include.

1. CONSCIOUSNESS-RAISING
2. CONSCIOUSNESS SENSITIZING
3. VALUES ANALYSIS
4. VALUES CLARIFICATION
5. VALUES CRITICISM
6. MORAL IMAGINATION
7. ETHICAL ANALYSIS
8. MORAL DECISION MAKING
9. RESPONSIBLE AGENTS
10. VIRTUE DEVELOPMENT
11. MORAL IDENTITY

Consciousness-raising is perhaps the easiest to accomplish
both in the classroom and outside: it happens to a freshman as
she meets her peers from other socioeconomic backgrounds, as
she takes introductory courses in the social sciences, as visiting
speakers alert her to the rape of our natural resources, or as she
gets involved in some student ministry. She becomes aware that
things in this world are not ideal; that people suffer from want
and prejudice and outright oppression; that administrative
procedures and structures in business and government, along
with ideological rigidity, can contribute to the problem rather
than alleviate it; that competitive power-mongering often takes
precedence over compassion and problem solving; that people
are hurting.

By then consciousness sensitizing is also occurring, as our
student begins to care, to feel compassion, to writhe at injustices.
It is a small step to the values analysis that tries to uncover the
effective values of those who are responsible for existing policies
or who make the decisions that affect people for better and for
worse. Values analysis can naturally occur in history, political
science, literature, and many of the humanities; it is akin to the

values clarification process in which I become aware of my own values, those which actually motivate what I do rather than the ones I self-righteously profess. Both values analysis and values clarification issue in values criticism that asks whether the operative values are what they ought to be. Therein we move from the descriptive task, revealing as that may be, to the normative.

To get beyond random criticism, however, and move in a more constructive direction, the first step must be to look beyond one's own reactions and feelings and to take what ethicists call "the moral point of view": that is, to think about situations not just self-interestedly but in universalizable terms. Since this is often a new experience, it takes imagination to think ethically, especially to do so with reference to theoretical principles. But moral imagination is also needed to trace the web of moral responsibilities that a situation entails, to envision various possible consequences, to come up with alternative game plans, and to define the real options.

Ethical analysis explores the various ingredients in a complex moral situation so as to assess available options and decide which is the morally best policy or action to pursue. This is where the carefully defined ethical principles of philosophers come in, along with their attention to logical procedures. Ethical analysis is not reducible to formal deductive reasoning, or to an algorithm to be followed. Rather, it requires extended interaction of ethical principles and other background beliefs with the facts in a case. In this interaction, knowing proper premises and having good reasoning skills alone are insufficient for reaching good moral decisions. It also requires virtues such as wisdom—that capacity for good judgment which is born of high principle—honest appraisal, well-digested experience, and imaginative insight. Decision-making models can identify the needed inputs that should feed into the process, but moral insight is deepened and enlivened by moral virtue.

Ethical analysis is needed in any field where moral dilemmas and other tough choices arise. This includes any area of business, anywhere personnel decisions are made, anywhere science and technology are put to use, anywhere human relations are involved, anywhere policies are being formulated or applied. By that token alone ethical analysis and decision making should to some extent be everybody's business.

Decisions lead to action. Moral education is accordingly concerned that students become consistent and responsible adults who care about other people, treat them justly, and do something about ethical issues in society. At an earlier stage in the history of higher education, proper personal behavior was the main and almost the only objective of moral education, and behavioral concerns are of course still reinforced by parental and constituency-related expectations in a small college. But a biblically oriented ethic points further than this and sees that how a person acts is related to her character. The development of specific virtues—what the Bible calls righteousness—is paramount, along with the integration of those virtues into that formed moral identity we call character. Among the many influences on character, the community in which one is a participant is utterly strategic, both for the role models it provides and for the values it embodies. Once again, then, ethics is clearly everybody's business.

We will return to these objectives in later chapters. But before we leave them, two concluding observations follow about moral education in the Christian college. *First,* we should distinguish it from the moralizing that simply inserts moral injunctions at every opportunity. Moralizing may be appropriate in early childhood, but hardly with young adults who are opening their eyes to the world of competing beliefs and values, and who are learning to think for themselves. Nor is it sufficient amid the increasing complexities of a fast-changing technological society. Students must learn to analyze what is going on, to understand themselves, to think through issues and make wise decisions based on principle, to be Christian through and through. Facilitating this, as we have been saying, is what constitutes moral education.

Second, we must distinguish education from indoctrination in this as in other aspects of learning. Indoctrination is a one-sided affair which, like thought control or brainwashing, does not give different points of view a fair hearing and so precludes informed and wise choices. In effect, it makes decisions for the student rather than teaching her to make decisions for herself. Whether by omission or caricature it distorts the facts; whether by psychological pressure or other not-so-subtle means it penalizes disagreement. On the other hand, ethics requires wise decisions, has to face the hardest facts, and must live with disagreement. Christians may well disagree on ethical matters, for in some situations there is no one clearly best solution. Indoctrination leaves the student unprepared for both the hard decisions and the moral ambiguities of life. But the teacher who knows his field and understands those ambiguities—the scientist, the psychologist, the historian, let us say—knows better. He owes his students a good education on the moral issues as well. Indoctrination is neither right nor safe. Moral education is the task.

Chapter Two

Assessing the Contemporary Climate

The environment in which we work is plainly important as we consider what objectives to emphasize or what methods to adopt. In the case of moral education we need to take stock of the social ethos out of which students come, the theological stance of the teacher and the college, and the processes of psychological growth through which students go. This three-fold environment comprises our starting place: in regards to the social environment, we focus on the present ethical climate; in regards to theology, the distinctive ethical emphases of different Christian traditions; in regards to psychology, theories of moral development.

THE PRESENT ETHICAL CLIMATE

DEAR ABBY: It is so difficult to know what is morally right and what is morally wrong these days. What used to be considered wrong 25 years ago is suddenly "right." How is a person supposed to know how to behave?

This simple complaint to the *Chicago Tribune* some years ago is all too familiar: we live in a world of changing values. But that is only part of the story, a symptom. In his-best selling indictment of today's universities, *The Closing of the American Mind,* Allan Bloom complains that students assume as if it were self-evident that truth is relative, and that their talk of differences in "life-style" or "sexual preference" implies that truth and falsity, right and wrong don't even exist. Values are reduced to subjective feelings rooted, if anywhere, in our individual biological makeups and psychological histories. Moreover, today's students, Bloom observes, are without any worldview that can ground values in reality. To what extent this social ethos characterizes Christian college students would be an interesting question for empirical research. How could it be absent in a shrunken world whose values are disseminated by pop music, mass media, and the entertainment and advertising industries? Students are certainly not insulated from such forces. They may have acquired a religious and moral language that seems to belie the charge of relativism or loss of worldview; yet their practice often reflects the relativism of our times. Even their language is individualistic and relativistic when they say something such as, "That may be right for him, but it wouldn't be right for me." Their commitment to service projects suggests a degree of altruism and social concern that we often read as high moral principle; but how much of that enthusiasm is a product of youthful exuberance and peer expectations is hard to say, particularly when these young activists later join the "Yuppie" generation.

Economic and social ambition, like the relativistic ethos, is doubtless fed by an exaggerated individualism that regards each of us as possessing an inalienable right to form and then pursue as our number one priority our own personal goals and values. My life is my own business—my goals, how I earn a living and spend my money, my sexual standards and overall lifestyle—provided only that I don't go around directly hurting other people. "Live and let live" is the motto, whether or not it is taken to a "me first" extreme. Robert Bellah and his associates amply documented this individualism in their *Habits of the Heart.* It has burgeoned today vastly beyond the Enlightenment assertion of a few individual rights in which democratic hopes are grounded.

11

The Old Testament picture is much more guarded. It is rather a picture of communities composed of individuals with shared commitments and values, pursuing God's purposes for them in this world. The New Testament plainly speaks of unchanging values intrinsic to the family, to governmental authority, to the workplace, and to the corporate life of the church. Any individualism that regards the pursuit of self-interest as top priority is by that standard morally wrong. And sin by any other name is still sin.

Yet relativism is also fed by the positivist mentality that grew from the rise of modern science, for it is there that values were separated from what is objectively real. Whereas both the Judeo-Christian worldview and the classical Greek tradition saw good ends inherent in nature's processes—and this agreement provided the basis for Western culture—a crucial change began when mechanistic science reduced nature to inert matter and blind forces, a world of value-free facts to be explained without reference to either intrinsic or transcendent purpose. Meanwhile human knowledge, it was insisted, must be objective, detached, value free. Auguste Comte and John Stuart Mill extended the empirical methods of natural science to the study of human behavior, social processes, and ethics. The result was that ethics became a utilitarian science of social management for our own ends. Twentieth-century positivists understandably came to the conclusion that normative value judgments about what ought to be or what is right and good are either generalizations about human attitudes or else just emotional outbursts that say nothing true or false at all. A value-free empirical world precludes our grounding of values in reality. But reducing value judgments to emotional outbursts means we really make no value judgments at all. You have your feelings and I have mine, and relativism can have its sway.

This, I suggest, is part of the social ethos that has influenced the student outlook on values. In philosophy generally, positivism and its emotivist theory are now passé. Yet in some disciplines and in our society at large it is still often assumed that nature is indifferent to human values, that values are just subjective feelings we impose on experiences, and that no other viable way of addressing value concerns is possible than by the cost-benefit methods that social and behavioral sciences afford. This is a day of therapists and social workers (and they are tremendously helpful), but not sufficiently a day of ethicists and theologians. Yet the assumption that nature is indifferent to human values is plainly challenged by a Christian view of God and his creation; and the assertion that only scientific knowledge counts ignores the rich resources not only of the humanities but also of both biblical revelation and more recent ethical theory. Nor is some form of utilitarianism the only option. The resources of natural law ethics, or a Kant-like respect for persons, or ethical intuitionism, or divine-command theories continue to be explored in the literature of both ethical theory and applied ethics. Since there is little justification for supposing that relativism and an uncritical authoritarianism are the only alternatives, moral education should make plain what other alternatives have to offer.

Moral education in today's social climate, then, requires both theological and philosophical literacy if it is to dispel the misconceptions that underlie value relativism and reintroduce thought about right and wrong and truth and falsity into decision making. Moral education is too large and complex a task and too involved with down-to-earth application to be left to theologians and philosophers alone, although they still have an essential role in laying adequate foundations and helping us to think informedly about what we believe.

DIFFERENCES IN THEOLOGY

While the ethical climate of the day affects student values, we must also be aware that different theological traditions lead to differing ethical emphases. Of course, the major Christian traditions hold a great deal in common: we share a dependency on Scripture and the kind of doctrinal affirmations contained in the Apostles' Creed with its trinitarian emphasis on God as creator, Christ's incarnation and triumph, and the work of the Holy Spirit in and through the church. And we agree on the necessity of both personal and social righteousness. Differences arose in historical situations as these essentials were more fully expounded and given application, differences that persist; a Christian college needs to draw on the particular ethical emphases of its own theological tradition while still learning from others.

Roman Catholic ethics, for instance, is greatly influenced by the natural law theory inherited from theologians like Thomas Aquinas—a kind of Christianized Aristotelianism. Basic to this natural law is the belief that every kind of created thing tends towards its God-given end, some good potential which it should ideally actualize. Self-preservation is a natural law evident even among inanimate things. Care for one's young is a natural law in the animal world. Among humans with their rationality and freedom of choice these become moral duties, duties ultimately to God. We ought to willingly embrace such natural ends and direct our actions towards them by thoughtful choice.

So suicide is morally wrong, and so are child abuse and child neglect. Since as humans we have the God-given capacity to order our lives rationally, we ought to seek wisdom and to prefer an ordered society governed by just laws for the common good. Catholic ethics, then, depends heavily on belief about how God orders his creation—that is, teleologically. Other aspects of Catholic theology also come into play. James Gustafson points out that because priests in the confessional have to respond to the specific actions of individuals, this practice has led to a casuistical treatment of moral issues.[1] And if we ask how progress is made in the moral life, then Catholic beliefs about how

---

1. James M. Gustafson, *Protestant and Roman Catholic Ethics: Prospects for Rapprochement* (University of Chicago Press, 1978), chap. 1.

divine grace is received come into play. The spiritual disciplines are important, as is participation in the sacraments.

Two key areas of theology thus emerge: how God orders his creation, and how divine grace is received. Creation and grace are common themes in all Christian traditions, but their manner of development differs in each tradition. A similar paradigm therefore applies when we turn to Reformed theology. John Calvin recognized a natural moral law more in the tradition of Roman jurisprudence influenced by Stoicism than in that of Aquinas, and he viewed the second half of the Decalogue as a reassertion of that moral law. His primary emphasis, however, was on the law of God given in Scripture. According to the Westminster Confession of Faith, obedience to moral law is mandatory for every human being out of respect for the authority of the Creator: the moral law is to be our rule of life, informing us of the will of God and of our duties as restorers and stewards of his creation. Reformed and Presbyterian liturgy accordingly still includes a biblical reading of the moral law. Classic Reformed theologies like Calvin's *Institutes of the Christian Religion* and Charles Hodge's *Systematic Theology* include extended expositions of the Decalogue, and ethicist Lewis Smedes has organized his recent *Mere Morality* around those commandments while emphasizing that they are rooted in human nature as God created it.

Where does grace come in? It comes through the Word and the sacraments. God's law has a threefold function: it reveals our sin, and it drives us to Christ, as well as providing a rule of life. The Holy Spirit so attends God's Word that it becomes a means to our repentance, forgiveness, and moral growth. And he so attends the sacrament, making the presence of Christ real to us in it, that it too becomes a means of grace. Creation and grace are thus the twin emphases in a Reformed ethic too.

In the case of Lutheran theology things are not as clearcut. The fundamental moral problem is not the need to know what we should do, but the ability to do it as we should. So while Luther's Larger Catechism contained an exposition of the Ten

Commandments, his main emphasis was on Christian liberty. As sinners we experience an inner bondage to sin that shows itself in self-absorption and blindness to the needs of others, in compulsiveness and overanxiety, in a paralyzing burden of guilt. But trust in God's grace liberates us from all of this, so that the justified can live by faith, freed to perform those ordinary tasks which are life's calling.

We live, therefore, with a tension between what the law requires that we fail to perform and the grace that forgives and frees sinners to pursue their callings. Amid moral conflicts we cannot resolve in a world where ideal options rarely arise—and even then our efforts tend to fail—grace helps us keep going. Where Calvinist theology has developed an ethic of obedience to God's sovereignty over every sphere of creation, the Lutheran emphasizes living within the conflict between God's kingdom and those of this world.

Anabaptist theology pursues this theme of living in a fallen world still further. Believers are called to be a separate community bearing witness by its life to another world that is yet to come. The emphasis is not on how God ordered his creation in the past, as if we have just to restore what was, but on the new creation, the kingdom which God's grace is bringing into being for the future. This discontinuity between the old and the new leads to an ethic of radical discipleship that avoids conforming to today's world, for only thereby can the witness be plain. Radical discipleship accepts suffering as part of the tension, and responds with a forgiving love that gives itself sacrificially for the needy and suffering of the world.

In Anabaptist moral education, therefore, the New Testament will receive most emphasis, and in it the example and teaching of Jesus in the Gospels. Philosophical ethics has much less place, since natural law, moral intuition, and the rule of reason are all ways of getting at a morality inherent in this present creation, rather than the new creation that is yet to be. Philosophical thinking can critique secular theories, teach logical reasoning, and nurture conceptual clarity, but it is not itself a source of moral guidance parallel to the Scriptures as it is for Catholic ethics and as it can be in Reformed thinking.

In that regard the Wesleyan tradition is closer to Thomism and to Reformed theology. Yet the distinctive theological emphasis is not on creation but on grace, more specifically on inner holiness. Christian perfection is the central theme, not in the sense of constantly flawless behavior but rather of a heart of perfect love for God. To love him with all my heart and soul is the first and greatest commandment, and to love my neighbor as myself is second only to that. A perfect heart means having pure intentions nurtured in intense spiritual experience. Yet Wesleyan piety does not confine its attention to the inner life in some self-absorbed manner: purity of intention leads to integrity of character and to social action.

Values education in the Wesleyan tradition will therefore be inseparable from the practice of piety. It will not rest content, however, with piety plus deliberation over moral decisions: it is more likely to focus on the ethics of virtue and on character formation as the natural outcome of a heart for God. In fact, Wesleyan theology reminds us all of the connection between moral development and personal spiritual growth, between ethics and piety, a connection almost totally ignored in the vast secular literature on both applied ethics and moral development.

For all our theological differences common themes about moral education persist: the importance of inner virtues as well as overt behavior, the inseparability of moral from spiritual development, and our need for both guidance and grace. Moral development thus becomes just one crucial facet of more holistic Christian growth and human development.

MORAL DEVELOPMENT THEORIES

Can education assist in the moral aspects of human development, and if so, how? How are nature and grace related in the process? If morality involves more than socially acceptable behaviors, then moral education involves more than socialization or legalistic approaches to behavior. Dissatisfaction with these behavioral approaches led to the values clarification movement with its emphasis on self-understanding and inner-directedness. While emphasis on the moral agent as a person was long overdue, by itself values clarification tended toward the relativism and individualism we have noted in the present social climate. We may well be reaping today the harvest of yesterday's attempts at behavioral change and the values-clarification movement that followed. We need a fuller approach to moral development than those attempts implied, one that includes critical thinking, not only *what* I really value but also *why*, and ways of thinking through an issue and deciding what really *ought* to be done. That will still be insufficient if moral growth includes doing and being as well as thinking, and if Christian character ultimately depends on divine grace. But cognitive aspects of moral development are still important and have been the subject of considerable empirical study, something which is still lacking in regards to character formation.

Prominent in these empirical studies of cognitive moral development is the work of the late Harvard psychologist, Lawrence Kohlberg.[2] Building on Piaget's structuralist approach Kohlberg conducted empirical studies resulting in a description of six stages in the development of moral reasoning. They fall into three levels.

Level I: Preconventional
Stage 1: Obedience based on consequences—"Will I be punished?"

---

2. See for example Kohlberg's *The Philosophy of Moral Development* (Harper and Row, 1981). For helpful Christian critiques, see Craig Dykstra, *Vision and Character: A Christian Education Alternative to Kohlberg* (Paulist Press, 1981), Donald M. Joy, *Moral Development Foundations: Judeo Christian Alternatives to Piaget-Kohlberg* (Abingdon Press, 1980), and Nicholas Wolterstorff, *Educating for Responsible Action* (Eerdmans, 1980).

Stage 2: Self-interest, hedonism—"What gives me most pleasure?"
Level II: Conventional
Stage 3: Seeking approbation—"Good boy!"
Stage 4: Law and order—"Follow the rules!"
Level III: Post-conventional
Stage 5: Utilitarian social contract—"Can we agree on a better way?"
Stage 6: A universal ethical principle, consciously adopted, and consistently applied.

An intervening stage was also suggested:

Stage 4½: Relativism, cynical of conventional standards.

William Perry claims this is a step towards ethical maturity in that it overcomes the "black-and-white" dualist mentality which allows no shades of gray, no moral ambiguities, and it leads in due course to ethical commitments of the sort represented by stage 6.[3] Note that the stage 4½ is not quite the same as Bloom's sense of relativism, where truth and falsity and right and wrong have no objective point of reference at all and don't even exist. Rather, Perry's is a relativism beset by moral ambiguity because of the difficulty in resolving disagreements about values. It is more like the relativism of the "Dear Abby" letter. While this might be compatible either with the denial of all objective truth or with the recognition that objective truth exists but is hard to find, the latter more naturally follows Perry's dualistic stage and admits the need for commitments which he emphasizes.

Since this kind of theory has become the paradigm for discussions of moral development and the teaching of ethics, some further comments are needed if we are to see what it contributes and where developmental studies need to be enlarged.

3. For example, *Forms of Intellectual and Ethical Development in the College Years* (Holt, Rinehart and Winston, 1970), pp. 9-10.

(1) *How helpful is it with college students?* Recent study shows that on Kohlberg's scale college freshmen are overwhelmingly at the conventional level, and seniors largely so as well. On Perry's scale, freshmen typically come to Christian colleges at a dualistic level, while seniors tend to be more relativistic—in Perry's sense, but not necessarily in Bloom's. Putting these findings together, we see that while our students encounter moral ambiguities and acknowledge reasoned disagreement, they still accept conventional positions rather than deciding independently on the commitments they make. This tells us where students are, and it could provide a basis for evaluating new efforts at moral education.

The further question arises of how to nurture growth. Kohlberg claims that the move to a higher stage is aided by "cognitive dissonance," a tension that comes from realizing that my present form of thinking cannot resolve an issue. Yet the Christian college environment, with its often unreflective acceptance of conventional Christian views and with its behavioral rules, plainly minimizes dissonance and encourages stages 3 and 4 thinking. And the rationales given for behavioral rules are either of the "law and order" type (stage 4) or else like a "utilitarian social contract" (stage 5). Somehow, cognitive dissonance must be created in the same context in which decisive commitment is encouraged. Issues must be raised which challenge uncritical thinking, so that teaching ethics will involve more than informative lectures about what biblical teaching and ethical theory say. Kohlberg calls for discussion of concrete case studies, dilemmas that compel the student to move beyond a "law and order" approach or a "relativist" paralysis of decision. Yet case studies require teachers whose moral concern and commitments, while not imposed on the student or the discussion, model the kind of outcome that is possible. Of this, more later.

(2) *The structuralist approach of Piaget and Kohlberg maintains that a universal pattern of cognitive development is programmed into us biologically.* Is it then the case that everybody must or does in fact follow the success stages in sequence without skipping a stage or

regressing to an earlier one? And *with what assurance can we measure these outcomes?* Empirical findings support the fact of regress, and my own unscientific observations of ethics students suggest that some seem to skip stage 5 (the "utilitarian social contract" approach) and make straight from stage 4's "law and order" toward the principle-oriented stage 6. Similarly, it would not be difficult to locate alumni who as students seemed to reflect stage 6 thinking but now, absorbed into a less principled society, function at stage 5 or even stage 4. Is this a case of regression? Or could it be that their collegiate thinking only *appeared* principled but was really approbation seeking (stage 3) or following rules (stage 4), so that principled thinking was never really internalized. Can we ever determine for sure which it is?

Genuine Christian conversion precipitates internalized changes in one's thinking, perhaps (or perhaps not) in its form but certainly in its content and goal, changes that at least point towards stage 6 (principled thinking) rather than stage 4 (conventional) or stage 5 (social contract), and so makes skipping a stage seem possible. Likewise, "backsliding" might precipitate regression to relativism. Yet the genuineness of principled reasoning may be just as uncertain to the teacher who leads a discussion or reads a student paper as is the genuineness of conversion to a pastor who hears a verbal affirmation. Granted the general pattern of growth Kohlberg proposes, then, we still remain unsure of where an individual really is on the scale, or where he will come out under the pressure of an ethically alien society. Internalized moral commitments, as I shall suggest later, show up more elsewhere than simply in the form our moral reasoning takes.

(3) *Is moral development a matter of nature or grace?* Kohlberg describes it as if it were a natural process, simply a matter of growing up. Is that a realistic enough assessment of human nature, handicapped as it is by the limitations of finitude and the bondage of sin? Is sin just immaturity?

But why must it be *either* nature *or* grace? On the one hand, if brain development is a precondition of cognitive development, and cognitive development is needed for growth in the kinds of moral reasons we give, then it follows that the theoretical abstraction needed for principled thinking is dependent on natural processes. So it may well be that college freshmen are at stage 3 or 4 because they are still psychologically incapable of further progress—they are insufficiently brain-developed. On the other hand, some people become principled moral thinkers who are not Christians: the literature in applied ethics (as well as biography and fiction) makes that obvious. And such thinking may well be prevented or at least handicapped not only by natural factors affecting intellectual ability and functioning, but also by human sinfulness. The kinds of inner bondage Luther referred to are very real in moral experience: self-absorption, blindness to the needs of others, and compulsiveness can at least temporarily blind us to moral principle. In that regard some people never grow up. What they need is the inner liberation that comes with conversion to Christ.

Immaturity, of course, is not the same as sin. Notably, Kohlberg's earlier stages do not focus on what is morally wrong: obedience, desire for pleasure and approbation, law and order, and social betterment by consensus are all good even if they are insufficient or not basic enough. They can be perverted, however, as can principled thinking, if one adopts as her universal principle some undeserving candidate. But the six stages may well trace the path that normal human development might naturally follow, though perhaps more speedily, spontaneously, and surely were it not for sin. In our fallen condition, it isn't that simple or sure.

(4) *Kohlberg's work only addresses one aspect of moral development,* namely, the *form* of moral reasoning. Some critics charge that even this is not characteristic of everybody: Carol Gilligan, for example, finds that women are not as oriented to objective rules and principled reasoning as men, but instead stress relationships and caring. It may be that this is simply a different way of saying the same thing, that rather than formulating rules to govern relationships or abstracting overall principles, their rules and principles are implicit in the way they relate and care. Alternatively, they may be less concerned with an ethic of duties

than with an ethic of virtue and personal character. In either case the differences may (or may not) be a product of thinking that is socialized by traditional sex roles: men made tough decisions at work and in government, while women traditionally assumed more interpersonal roles in the community and at home.

Gilligan's objection cannot be easily dismissed. Similar concerns surface when we observe that Kohlberg individualizes moral development as if thinking goes on privately, alone, rather than as a dynamic in the relationships that go on in a community. An individualistic view of the human person is taken for granted by Kohlberg, rather than a relational view such as I suggested earlier and Gilligan seems to prefer. Relationships are not just cognitive but also very much affective. And if personal and moral development goes on in relationship to others—if we are through and through relational beings—then the affective as well as the cognitive dimensions of moral growth require attention. Consider the effect of marriage or parenthood on a young man's ability to accept responsibility. Consider the contribution of a support group when one is making tough decisions. Consider the effect of conversion to Christ and of membership in his body, the church. Principled decisions and behaviors are not always dependent on stage 6 reasoning: on the contrary, while such moral reasoning is sometimes invaluable in decision making and while it may well mark one kind of growth, yet it is neither necessary nor sufficient in deciding and acting on principle. We must therefore be careful to incorporate emphases other than moral reasoning alone into moral education and into evaluating moral development.

(5) *Is the form of thinking the only cognitive concern?* Is not the content of moral thinking a concern as well? Kohlberg is a Kantian here, with a concept of justice that emphasizes equal individual rights, so that he emphasizes moral dilemmas in which conflicts of rights occur. But are *all* moral problems requiring thoughtful decisions reducible to rights problems? Is that conception of justice sufficiently biblical? Plainly, the Old Testament view of justice speaks to the *needs* of the poor as well

23

as the *rights* of the oppressed, so that issues of justice and issues of love seem inseparable, and the affective and cognitive dimensions of ethics merge.

But by reducing justice to equal rights, Kohlberg separates it from love and diminishes the scope of moral concern that is needed. In Christian principled thinking I may choose to forego a right when asking what both justice and love require, or what the poor and oppressed may need. Perhaps Gilligan is closer to this kind of principled reasoning than even she supposed.

Kohlberg's principled stage of reasoning is really an Enlightenment kind of ethic with individualistic assumptions. It is an Enlightenment ethic also in its emphasis on action decisions and reasoning from principles. It is the kind of ethic which Alasdair MacIntyre's *After Virtue* critiqued in contrast to an ethic of virtue rooted in both the Greek and the biblical tradition. At the least we must say that Kohlberg's moral-development theory shares the limitations of Enlightenment ethics. Moral reasoning skills may be important, but they are not enough for all that a Christian ethic involves, both in content and in regard to responsible agency and moral character.

James Rest presents a more holistic picture, one that better fits the range of objectives for moral education introduced in our last chapter, when he proposes a research model that delineates four components essential to moral behavior.[4]

1. Moral sensitivity—recognizing how people are affected by an action. (Cp. our objectives 1 and 2, consciousness raising and sensitizing.)
2. Moral judgment—formulating an ideal course of action in a particular situation. (Cp. objective 7, ethical analysis.)
3. Moral choice—putting moral values ahead of personal interests. (Cp. objectives 6 and 8, moral imagination and decision.)
4. Moral action—implementing moral intentions by plan-

---

4. James R. Rest, *Moral Development: Advances in Research and Theory* (Praeger, 1986), chap. 1.

ning with ego strength, social skill, and maturity. (Cp. objective 9, responsible agency.)

Rest thus insists that moral development is not just cognitive, that the cognitive is never devoid of the affective nor the affective of the cognitive, but rather that they are inseparably interwoven throughout. Moreover, his four components are not sequential stages of development; far more complex interactions occur.

The same is true of our eleven objectives. They are not a disconnected potpourri devoid of any structure; under closer examination they fall into three groups focussing respectively on the conscience, on decision making, and on moral character.

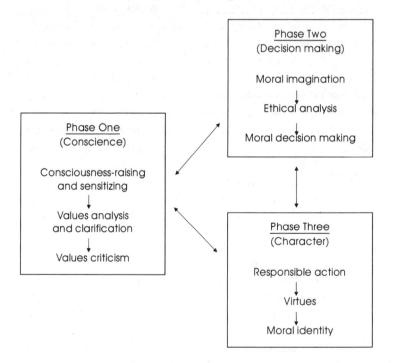

Here then are three phases in moral education (see above). The first moves from consciousness-raising to the critical appraisal of one's values. That in turn leads in two parallel directions: to phase two, where imagination and reasoning skills are applied to moral decisions; and to phase three, with its more whole-personal emphasis on responsible action, virtue, and moral identity. But they are not strictly sequential, for while the formed conscience both informs moral decisions and guides the development of character, decision making and character development are mutually influential; and principled decisions both contribute to shaping character and are shaped by it. In addition, they both feed back into the refinement of values. This is the kind of interaction James Rest would affirm.

Here then are three factors affecting moral education: the present ethical climate, the variety of theological traditions, and moral development theory. But it now becomes evident that these three are themselves interrelated, for Kohlberg's theory reflects the ethical assumptions of our day, while lacking important theological insights. To address moral education adequately, therefore, we need an understanding of moral development informed both by a thorough critique of the contemporary ethos (an exercise in values analysis and criticism), and by the broader objectives and dynamics of a theologically aware Christian ethic.

Chapter Three

Forming the Conscience

We turn now to phase one: consciousness-raising and sensitizing, values analysis and clarification, and values criticism. Together they shape the conscience. The biblical notion of conscience does not imply that we are given an innate moral code common to all human beings, as popular usage sometimes suggests. It is rather a conscious sensitivity (the French for "consciousness" *is* "conscience") that needs to be informed, sharpened, and directed, but that also can be dulled and misinformed. It can either accuse or excuse (Rom. 2:14-15), but it may also be weak (I Cor. 8:7, 12), seared (I Tim. 4:2), or defiled (Titus 1:15). Since conscience needs to be both sensitive and rightly informed, moral education has both affective and cognitive objectives.

This is where *values* come in: they inform the conscience. The term "value" has a twofold meaning: as a verb, "to value" something is to prize or desire it; as a noun, a "value" is what we prize or desire. So values education will concern itself both with the appropriateness of values and with people's sensitivity concerning them.

As Albert Einstein once put it:

> It is essential that the student acquire an understanding of and a lively feeling for values. He must acquire a vivid sense of the

beautiful and the morally good. Otherwise he—with his specialized knowledge—more closely resembles a well-trained dog
than a harmoniously developed person.[1]

The word "values" is often used quite loosely to include
beliefs, preferences, and assumptions of any sort. I am confining
it to what we regard as ideals: ends we desire, regard as good,
and think we ought to pursue. We talk not only of moral values
like honesty, but also of political values like justice, social values
like friendship, intellectual values like understanding, and so
forth. There are moral dimensions to these other values, and if
they are indeed good ends we have a moral responsibility to
pursue them. To remain willfully ignorant where understanding
is needed, or to go around destroying valued friendships, is
morally blameworthy. Furthermore, *how* we seek justice or pre-
serve liberty, conduct our research or treat our friends, are all
moral matters. Moral ends are called for in every area of life, as
well as moral means to those ends. So while the variety of values
includes more than purely moral ones, moral values pervade
them all. No area of life is value free, and none is wholly amoral.

Right values, then, are good ends of various sorts. As such
they represent objective possibilities for good that are inherent
in life. While this may appear obvious—a truism—it nonetheless points up one difference between Christians (and other
theists) and many naturalists. A Christian value theory begins
where the Apostles' Creed begins, with God the creator. The
value judgment in the Genesis narrative ("good . . . good . . .
very good") underscores the fact that God created in line with
his own good ends, making the world and humankind with
inherent possibilities for all sorts of good that he wants to see
realized. That is why understanding is possible, friendship is
possible, knowing God is possible: they are good ends inherent
in how we are made, values God wants us to pursue.

The naturalist, on the other hand, who sees the world and

1. Albert Einstein, *Ideas and Opinions,* ed. Carl Seelig and others,
trans. by S. Borgmann (Crown Publishers, 1954), p. 64.

human nature as products of chance in a purposeless world, recognizes no inherent values, but only those which we ourselves create and choose to pursue. Hence the relativist tendency. On the other hand, the unrealistic romanticist, overly idealistic about life, tends to exaggerate the goodness of things as they currently are, as if we live in a world of fully achieved (or at least fully achievable) ideals. The Christian will be more realistic than that, knowing how human finiteness and sin can keep us from both desiring and achieving the ends to which we should properly aspire. Yet we have more hope than a naturalist who sees the world as value neutral—indifferent to what is good—more hope because of possibilities God created and that his saving grace both renews and extends.

Moral values are only one kind of values, then, but they are inseparably intertwined with other kinds; and what we in fact value, individually and as a society, needs careful scrutiny and realignment with God's good ends for his creatures. This is what phase one in moral education, the forming of a conscience, is about: sensitivity to and a realignment of right values.

I speak of "realignment" rather than "reconsideration" because developing a conscience must go beyond a purely cognitive examination of value concepts to the affective aspects of *valuing*. To understand and correct a conception of justice is not enough: we must also *love* justice and pursue it. Values clarification advocates were right that choosing, cherishing, and acting are what valuing involves. But can moral education expect affective as well as cognitive outcomes?

John Stuart Mill thought it worth trying, if only for utilitarian reasons.

> If we wish men to practice virtue, it is worth while trying to make them love virtue, and feel it as an object in itself, and not a tax paid for leave to pursue other objects. It is worth training them to feel not only actual wrong or actual meanness, but the absence of noble aims and endeavours, as not merely blameable but also degrading: to have a feeling of . . . the poorness and insignificance of human life if it is all spent in making things comfortable

for ourselves and our kin, and raising ourselves and them a step or two on the social ladder.[2]

On the cognitive side, it is obviously important in the Christian college to identify biblical values and their present relevance and to emphasize, as I have just done, the theistic basis for values. Equally high on the agenda is an emphasis on the theocentric unity of values: if glorifying God and enjoying him forever is indeed our highest end, then all other ends derive their value from that. But we must also underscore the human nature of valuing, how our finiteness and our fallenness keep us from valuing what and how we ought, as well as from fully achieving those good ends in this life. As Luther stressed, the just who live by faith depend on God's mercy as they pursue the good.

Understanding these things puts values in theological context. But it also has affective power in illuminating and energizing inner struggles of conscience. The truth can make us free. Anyone who takes seriously the role of Scripture in spiritual growth knows this is so; it pierces like a sword into the thoughts and intents of the heart; so does the truth about our sin and God's grace. Cognitive as well as affective dimensions of moral education, it must be remembered, are furthered by the witness of the Holy Spirit. The point is that values cannot be imposed from the outside but must be assimilated inwardly: moral indoctrination is a contradiction in terms and so is the legislation of values. Forming right values requires the inner development of a hearty love for God's good purposes in his creation.

Further insight comes from rejecting the individualistic view of persons that arose in the Enlightenment in favor of the more biblical picture of our interrelatedness in families and communities. Values, especially right values, do not develop effectively within an unrelated individual in isolation from

2. "Inaugural Address at St. Andrews," Feb. 1, 1867, in *The Six Great Humanistic Essays of John Stuart Mill* (Washington Square Press, 1963), p. 313. Quoted by Earl McGrath in "Careers, Values and General Education," *Liberal Education* 60 (Oct. 1974): 290.

people and communities, but in interpersonal and social contexts with all the loyalties they engender. So God set us in families and calls us into the community of faith where the good ends inherent in creation and grace are lovingly pursued.

Values education must keep this in mind. The individualistic approaches of both values clarification techniques and Kohlberg's cognitive development will not be enough, for values are shared and formed in interpersonal relationships; they bond relationships into communities, and they are pursued in community with others. The classroom is an insufficient context, therefore, for what we want; the entire life of the college community is involved, and more.

LEARNING TO CARE

A woman educator who heard me refer to conscience formation remarked that she well remembers when she first *heard* of "the women's problem" and then, in distinction, when she first *saw* it all around her and began to *feel* its weight.

To have a conscience about something is to care about it. This affective nature of conscience suggests that we do well to start with life situations that will both awaken reflection and stir feeling. The relational nature of persons suggests that these be interpersonal and social situations with which students can identify. Consciousness-raising and sensitizing, while very minimal objectives, can meet this twofold criterion. Meanwhile, it takes little imagination to find ways of exposing students to social problems that pose ethical questions. Objectionable business practices, public-policy decisions, manipulative advertising, unscrupulous ghetto landlords, street people, unaffordable medical care, world hunger, the influence of technology, pollution of natural resources, and a myriad of other concerns are always in the news. Movies and novels and campus life, in addition to more traditional course

31

material, provide further means for raising awareness of values at work.

Some colleges have attempted all-campus consciousness-raising events. Students have voted to go without a meal, the proceeds going to meet some crucial human need. Student summer projects have alerted the entire student body to third-world needs. An all-campus "Moral Issues Day" has brought speakers and offered discussion groups or seminars. A two-day "Ethics Workshop" highlighting some issue brings scholars together with practitioners and students, ethicists with business people, social workers, and perhaps a beneficiary of some model program that addresses a concrete problem. These are co-curricular efforts with a potentially broad influence.

Firsthand encounters tend to arouse sympathy and concern, so that a sensitizing process begins. A field trip can leave the student feeling like an outside observer, for some situations are so alien to her experience that she feels distant, or perhaps they are so unpleasant as to seem hideous or painful to behold. She feels revulsion rather than compassion. One of my colleagues, a sociologist, consequently adopts a method of "voluntary displacement": he has students locked up in the county jail for a couple of days, searched and processed and treated like common felons. He has them become "street people," living and sleeping with the homeless on the sidewalks of Chicago. Overcoming the paralysis of revulsion, they soon feel genuine compassion and want to do something to help.

The moral psychology behind such a method seems sound, for, as David Hume pointed out, we feel sympathy and talk of injustice because we identify with people like ourselves in their pain; voluntary displacement enables even privileged white middle-class young people to identify with the needy. Consciousness sensitizing most readily results when one comes to feel *with* those in need. In that sense it is a function of shared experiences, of some real relatedness to others.

Yet consciousness-raising cannot be only at the affective level. The teacher should provide debriefing that helps the student process her experience and think informedly about it. As the Hastings Center report on *The Teaching of Ethics in Higher Education* puts it,

> Our feelings of sorrow, pity, anguish, or outrage may be delivering true messages. But they can never be taken utterly for granted, and the minimal perception to be conveyed to students is the possible difference between what they feel at first to be right or good and what they later conclude.[3]

The conscience needs to be properly informed.

We should not underestimate the role of family and friends in both raising the level of moral consciousness and informing the conscience. Conversations about concerns in today's world provide eye-openers; habitual sayings, like the proverbial wisdom of the Old Testament community, reinforce an awareness of values. "A job that's worth doing at all is worth doing well," my mother habitually said when I was a child—and it has stayed with me ever since. "It's always too soon to quit," President Edman of Wheaton College used to say—and generations of students carried that slogan away with them. "Wisdom is better than jewels," wrote Solomon, words to which our own acquisitive society should be more sensitive today.

I still recall the impression made on me as an undergraduate by an inscription on a bust of the college's founder, a quotation from a speech he gave in 1839:

> A perfect state of society is . . . where what is right in theory exists in fact, where practice coincides with principle and the law of God is the law of the land.[4]

Such words, read again and again, impress ideals on the conscience.

---

3. *The Teaching of Ethics in Higher Education* (Hastings Center, 1980), p. 49.

4. Jonathan Blanchard, later the first president of Wheaton College, in a speech at Oberlin College.

THE WHYS BEHIND OUR CHOICES

Moral education must go beyond awareness of ideals and feelings of compassion and even a compulsion to act. We need to
think about how values operate in the everyday world of the
slum landlord and the angry tenant, the second generation
welfare recipient as well as the policy maker, the juvenile of-
fender, the inside trader on the stock market. This is where
values analysis comes into play.

Take an obvious case from television advertising by auto-
mobile dealers. Here is a couple in evening dress, she be-
jewelled, wearing expensive furs, sliding into the leather seats
of some prestigious limousine. Or an attractive girl with obvious
sex appeal, caressing a convertible while she eyes you sugges-
tively. What considerations are given weight? How are choices
being addressed? What values are appealed to?

Richard Morrill proposes uncovering the values at work
in a situation by asking leading questions:

> What patterns of behavior do you see?
> What priorities do these patterns reveal?
> What factors are therefore given weight, and what are
>   excluded? What is sacrificed for the sake of what?
> On what basis are choices made or justified?
> What alternative paths of action are available?
> What values are inherent in each?[5]

The questions are well chosen: behavior *patterns* reveal
priorities; choices involve alternative *outcomes,* all of which are
value laden. Considerations like these make one conscious of
people's goals, the ends they prefer and which they really value
despite what they may profess to the contrary.

This method is needed in examining professional and

5. Adapted from Richard Morrill, *Teaching Values in College* (Jossey-
Bass, 1980), p. 80.

34

corporate codes of ethics, if we are not to adopt them uncritically. The journalism or speech teacher whose classes study famous speeches or current debates finds it a natural approach. The literature teacher handling a Walker Percy novel could hardly avoid it; so too the political scientist or sociologist discussing public policy. I think of a history teacher who systematically looks at historical case studies this way, and of a writing teacher who has developed exercises to show the relation of word choice and syntax to values, for even linguistic habits are value laden.

But the student is liable to turn the skills he thus acquires on his mentors, on curricular decisions, course structures, pedagogical methods, admissions policies, business office procedures, and a host of other features in college administration and teaching. What educators really value most may or may not be the values they profess and try to teach, yet the student who learns to uncover values will soon begin to see what they really prize. *How* they teach values may even be counterproductive to *what* values they try to teach, and curricular endeavors may well be hampered by institutional and community practices. Embodying values is often much more effective than talking about them.

Values analysis applies to current, historical, and fictitious situations; a kind of approach the values clarification movement developed to help people uncover their own values. Values clarification expert Sidney Simon is explicit that choices, priorities, and behavior patterns reveal underlying inner values; they define "full values" in relation to:

Choosing freely
Choosing among alternatives
Choosing after reflection
Prizing and cherishing
Affirming publicly
Acting on one's choice
A pattern of actions that is repeated.

35

Other "value indicators" they list, while less definitive than the above, include aspirations, attitudes, interests, feelings, beliefs, worries, and problems.[6]

Values clarification tries to help people look at their own lives and see what their own values really are. The method is simple: by discussion, role-playing, or in response to something the person says or does, introduce a clarifying question or comment that will stimulate reflection and evoke self-understanding: "Why do you prefer this?" or "You seem to be after something else." The method goes beyond merely addressing behaviors and putting a premium on conformity; it sees morality as rooted inwardly in *why* we make the choices and do the things we do. Self-understanding is essential to knowing that "why," and thence to inner growth.

An analogous procedure is evident in some of Jesus' conversations. His response to the rich ruler led that young man to see what he most loved (Luke 18:18-24). His repeated questions to Peter after the resurrection, "Do you love me more than these? . . . do you love me?" served a similar purpose. Self-understanding is essential to genuine commitment. The kind of heart searching elicited by values-clarification procedures can thus contribute to the choice between two masters, between two roads, between God and mammon, between the spirit and the flesh. It can lead to confession of sin and to coveting earnestly the best gifts. The biblical ideal of righteousness can be furthered by clarifying the values we actually embody, consciously or not, and resetting our affections. Choosing! Reflecting! Cherishing! Public affirmation! Acting on our choices! A pattern or lifestyle that persists! In those regards values clarification is targeted aright.

The problem with the values clarification movement was that it seemed to limit itself to a process without content, growth without direction. Since no values were advocated other than the values inherent in the process itself, it was criticized for

---

6. Sidney Simon, *Meeting Yourself Halfway: Thirty-One Values Clarification Strategies for Daily Living* (Argus Communcations, 1974), p. xv.

taking a relativist and individualistic position as if one's heritage and the values of the community are irrelevant, and as if good values somehow naturally emerge in the process of life. By itself it seemed an inadequate alternative to ethical indoctrination or behavioral conformity: too uncritical, too incomplete, too ethically limited.

Values criticism is needed to weigh alternative values, to explore assumptions and the worldviews in which values are rooted, and to introduce more normative questions. That something *is* valued does not imply it *ought* to be valued. What "ought" to be must come into moral education as well.

DECIDING WHAT MATTERS

Values, according to our definition, are ends we desire and pursue; right values are God's good ends for his creation. In a Christian context this must be the point of reference. If we are discussing values in the workplace or the business community we need to ask about the meaning and the proper purposes for economic activity, and to examine the values currently operative in that light. In regards to sexual behavior, the meaning and purpose of sex and marriage must come into play. In regards to public policy, beliefs about the purpose of government are crucial. These critical inputs are what, in another context, Nicholas Wolterstorff has called "control beliefs."[7] In other contexts they have been labelled "background beliefs" and "middle level concepts." A Christian's control beliefs here are about God's purposes, the good he intends for areas of life common to humankind, like work, sex, government, health, or friendship. For anyone who believes values are theistically grounded, values criticism must involve some such standard.

Consider these contrasting definitions:

7. *Reason within the Bounds of Religion* (Eerdmans, 1976), chap. 9.

Judeo-Christian Value	Contrasting Value
1. Value of power over individuals as service to help others develop unique gifts (Phil. 2:1-18; John 13:1-4).	Value of power over individuals as domination and control of others.
2. Value of power over nature as a stewardship by persons over God's world. Persons are called to the whole of creation (Gen. 1:26-31).	Value of power over nature as a mandate to produce a maximum of consumer goods and creature comforts.
3. Value of wealth and property as opportunity for increased service for humankind, yet as a possible obstacle to salvation (Luke 16:19-31; Luke 12:13-21; Mark 12:41-44).	Value of wealth and property as the measure of a person's worth.
4. Value of happiness as achieved through following God's intentions for humankind (Mark 8:36).	Value of happiness as achieved through acquiring possessions.
5. Value of justice as the right of each person to the means of leading a human life (Acts 2:42-47; Lev. 25:1-55; Gal. 3:27-28).	Value of justice as the protection of property already possessed.
6. Value of deferring gratification of wants (John 12:23-26; Luke 14:27; Matt. 16:24; Matt. 10:39).	Value of immediate gratification.
7. Value of time as reverence for God (Luke 12:22-32).	Value of time as money.[8]

8. F. Williams and J. W. Houck, *Full Value* (Harper and Row, 1978), p. 24.

In each case, some biblical control belief is at work, with the result that wealth and power, for example, have lower priority than where values are not formed by Judeo-Christian beliefs.

This is not simply a matter of labelling values as Christian or non-Christian. It is not that easy: an ethical issue hinges more often on the impact of biblical control beliefs on the ranking of values in their proper order of importance. Pedagogically it is essential that the student learn to work with those beliefs by asking what work (or government or whatever value area) is ultimately about, and so discover the adequacy or inadequacy of values under consideration. Are they biblically consistent? Are they sufficiently comprehensive? Can they apply to a larger world of adult responsibilities? How do they come together in a coherent way that gives overall purpose to life? How do they relate to the highest good—what the catechism calls "the highest end of man"? Values criticism of this sort is provoked and values are shaped not so much by isolated biblical texts as by what the Bible as a whole says about major areas of life's responsibilities, by biblical theology of work, or sex, or government. It then becomes not just a negative activity, but a constructive activity that instills biblical ideals into our thinking.

With values formation, as with consciousness-raising, interpersonal relationships are a major influence. Parents are usually the initial conveyers of values, then the peer group takes their place during the growing independence of adolescence. This makes residence-hall life strategic. Teachers sometimes play a role, whether as parent figures or by identifying with students as "would-be peers." Values, not just verbalized but truly incarnated, are catching. This accounts for the influence of a community with its shared values, like the family, the church, the fraternity or club, even the small college community as a whole. It accounts for how the humanities influence people's values—especially literature with its imaginative creation of characters, relationships, and experiences into which the reader is drawn empathetically and transported into a world other than her own. Even values incarnated in literature can be catching.

Similarly, the consciousness sensitizing of students exposed to the homeless on inner-city streets may lead to self-giving service in a shelter or clinic, an investment of time, energy, and emotion that reinforces inwardly the values which their outward behaviors profess, the more so the more habitual it becomes. Serving other people affects our values.

Finally, the Christian college must recognize that worship freely and sincerely given relates to values too. Notice how well it embodies the criteria that the values-clarification movement set forth:

> We choose among alternatives (in worshipping the one whom alone we should serve).
> We choose after reflection (in hearing the Word of God).
> We prize and cherish (in adoration and praise).
> We publicly affirm (in a corporate confession of faith).
> We adopt a repeated behavioral pattern (in the liturgy and form of worship we employ).

Worship of God acclaims him as our highest end, who makes every other good end worthwhile. Worship, freely and habitually enjoyed in a community of the committed, is therefore at the heart of conscience formation. In the Christian college where worship is taken for granted, routinized, attendance perhaps required, it too easily becomes hackneyed, trivialized, powerless. Moral education in the Christian college will be seriously compromised without the scrutiny and integration of a student's values that meaningful worship affords. Phase one, with its focus on values, accordingly points us in two directions. One leads from the cognitive functions of values criticism to ethical analysis and decision making; the other leads from the affective assimilation of improved values and the shaping of conscience to the formation of character. To the former of these, the second phase of moral education, the next chapter turns.

Chapter Four

Making Moral Decisions

A sensitive conscience informed by right values is a necessary precondition for making good moral decisions in difficult situations, but it is not sufficient. Many of the decisions that confront us are not simple questions of right and wrong, and the classic moral syllogism applies only to the simplest cases where decisions are more a matter of recognition rather than of reasoning.

> Lying is wrong.
> Falsifying your income on tax returns is lying.
> Therefore, falsifying your income on tax returns is wrong.

Of course it is! We don't need a syllogism to tell us it is wrong. A sensitive conscience is all it takes to make that judgment. But are the borders of lying always that clear? And is lying invariably wrong? What about a feint in playing football, or undercover work by the F.B.I., or pretending not to hear a pesky remark? What about deceiving Gestapo agents looking for the Jew in your attic? Are these all lying? Are they all wrong?[1] Sometimes moral dilemmas arise in which no altogether good

---

1. On the ethical complexities of lying, see Sisilla Bok, *Lying* (Vintage Books, 1979).

option exists—in medical ethics or political policy or military action, for example. These not-so-simple situations call for analysis that goes beyond an intuitive recognition of right and wrong. Not everything is black and white: shades of gray abound, morally ambiguous situations confront us, and we need to live wisely with ambiguity in a complex and fallen world. It takes imagination and analytic skills to make difficult decisions well.

MORAL IMAGINATION

I was talking with a retired army officer when the conversation turned to the morality of nuclear weapons: he seemed unable to think in other terms than that war has always involved the slaughter of innocent people. "Just war" concerns like the proportionality of force, reasonable hope of success, and the immunity of noncombatants from direct attack had no place in his thinking. He was not accustomed, at least in his professional field, to taking the moral point of view. For many people this is a new experience and one to which we do not readily take.

Other examples quickly spring to mind: middle-level managers bent at all costs on advancement up the corporate ladder; the white-collar criminal motivated by greed, who thinks only of how much he can get away with; the computer whiz kid who loves to break into confidential files; teenagers out for a good time who never stop to think either of the expense to taxpayers of their wild pranks, or of the effect on their parents, or the costly education they are shortchanging. None of these are looking at what they do from the moral point of view. The shift from self-interest or just plain thoughtlessness would be like stepping into another world, at least another way of thinking. It takes imagination to see things that differently.

It takes still more imagination to recognize the wide and complex web of responsibilities in a particular case, and to anticipate all the different kinds of possible consequences. Yet good decision making requires that of us, and more. It requires a sensitive conscience, an empathetic kind of insight into the effects our actions have on others, the capacity to identify with what they experience; it means imagining what it must be like to be in their shoes. All this is prerequisite to genuine caring, to compassion, to seeking what is just. Then it takes still more imagination to come up with alternative game plans, to see their potential consequences and how they might affect people's lives. Moral imagination is indispensable in analyzing a complex moral situation and coming up with a good decision.

Nurturing imagination is by no means a new objective for either parents or teachers. We start playing games with our children as soon as they are able to imitate or make any meaningful response. We tell them stories, show them pictures, expose them to all sorts of different experiences. Developing moral imagination is in principle no different: discovering the complexities of moral decisions is like reading a good mystery story and trying to identify the culprit. Novels and plays, films and videos, historical and other scenarios we might construct all help develop the imagination. And exposure to actual case study discussions, a staple diet of ethics instruction, plays this role as well.

ETHICAL ANALYSIS

Complex moral situations call for a methodical kind of analysis, for some structure to our thinking. As a step in that direction, distinguish four levels of attention: bases, principles, rules, and cases.[2] Discussion usually begins with particular cases, from which we back up to area rules, whether commonly accepted

2. For further elaboration, see A. F. Holmes, *Ethics: Approaching Moral Decisions* (InterVarsity Press, 1984), chap. 6.

moral guidelines, a professional code of ethics, or biblical injunctions for a given area of responsibility like truth telling or safeguarding human life. When no such rules exist that apply to a case in question, or when they pose conflicting obligations which cannot all be met, then we turn to overall moral principles underlying all moral rules. When those overall principles are questioned, discussion focusses on the philosophical and/or religious bases in which morality is ultimately grounded.

This fourfold analysis is evident in biblical ethics as well. A myriad of particular *cases* arise in the historical and prophetic books of the Old Testament, and the Mosaic code includes case laws—rules for typical kinds of cases, like finding someone's lost livestock or returning borrowed clothing. Case laws are more specific applications of *area rules,* such as the second half of the Ten Commandments which address universal areas of human responsibility: the sanctity of human life, of personal property, of marriage, and of truth. Thus, returning lost or borrowed property respects the owner's moral right to what he has legally acquired, and so respects his labor. Area rules in their turn, as the Hebrew prophets repeatedly remind us, reflect overall moral *principles* like love and justice, the ideals of a kingdom yet to come in its fulness, a kingdom of *shalom* where justice, love, economic sufficiency and human well-being of every sort flourish. All this has its *basis* in the purposes God has for his creation, just as the possibility of achieving justice for all depends on his grace and power.

This fourfold distinction responds to a well-intentioned objection to moral reasoning, posed as a question: "But what of God's will in the matter?" God's will is the *basis* of Christian ethics; how we *know* what God's will may be is a further question, one that principles and rules address. Likewise, simple appeals for love and justice do not tell us what ought to be done in any particular case, for love and justice are *overall* moral concerns that need specific application in various areas of life. Distinguishing basis, principles, rules, and cases helps us organize our thinking more clearly about the part each kind of consideration plays.

With this in mind, then, consider the inputs needed in working towards a moral decision in a particular case. (1) First, we need to be clear about all *the relevant facts*. Take, for example, the well-known Manville Asbestos case in which a company failed to inform its employees of the health hazards of working in its plant. Notice the wide range of relevant facts required in assessing responsibility:

> How serious were the risks to health?
> What evidence existed at the time?
> Was the company fully aware of these risks?
> Was the lack of warning due to negligence or was it a deliberate deception?
> Who was ultimately responsible?
> What did he do or not do, and why?
> Could the risks have been reduced or eliminated?
> What efforts were made to reduce the risks?
> Could the company eliminate the risk and stay in business?
> Were government safety standards violated? If so, why was this not caught?
> Were any contractual rights violated?
> What was the company response as health problems became evident?

Questions such as these attempt to get at the extent and causes of the problem, at who were responsible and what their intentions and loyalties were. A kind of values analysis takes place such as was discussed in the previous chapter. Consideration of the facts in a case thus includes both the facts and the values they reveal.

(2) A second kind of input has to do with *moral rules and responsibilities*. Continuing with the Manville example:

> What legal and contractual obligations existed?
> What company policies were in force?
> What moral expectations existed in the company?

Is there a corporate code of ethics? Any industry-wide consensus, either written or tacit?

What employee rights may have been violated?

What explicit guidelines or regulations are needed for the future?

Notice that moral obligations in an area like safety standards may include not only contractual and governmental regulations but also tacit moral expectations that may not have been officially spelled out by a society or business. Moral obligations, as moral education must constantly stress, extend significantly beyond legal obligations: legal obligation rests on a consensual morality and includes only what is enforceable; a Christian ethic, and indeed many another ethical position, addresses matters on which a consensual social ethic is silent. So moral education in a Christian context will add to the questions we have asked about moral rules in the Manville case:

What pertinent policies should Christians in management work to have their companies adopt?

(3) To evaluate existing rules, regulations, and policies, or to develop new ones, we appeal to a third input, the *broader moral principles* that apply in every area of human responsibility; it is here that ethical theories of a philosophical sort can come into play. This may be seen in the rich literature available on virtually every area of applied ethics. The utility principle, that we should act to maximize the surplus of good over evil for the maximum number of people, lays emphasis on consequences. The Kantian principle, that we should always treat people as ends of value in themselves and not just as means to our own ends, obligates us to certain duties independent of the consequences. While we are responsible for the consequences of our actions, policies, and rules, we are *not only* responsible for the consequences; we must also respect other persons—the Christian adds this because she recognizes we are all made in the image of God.

46

Theological ethics will emphasize as overall principles the great commandment to love as Christ loves us, or the prophetic injunction to do justice and love mercy. While justice and love are the overarching ethical concerns of Scripture, care must be taken to ensure that they are properly understood. The biblical *agape* is a self-giving love, to be carefully distinguished from loving in the sense of "liking" or "desiring," even though *agape* can infuse, purify, and change our likes and desires. Similarly, biblical justice is not to be equated with the eighteenth-century view of protecting individual rights, because it is a more communitarian concept requiring compassion and a social order that is equitable and benefits even the poor.[3]

These principles provide input in thinking about cases like the Manville example.

> Was sufficient attention paid to the predictable consequences of allowing health hazards to continue unchecked?
>
> Employees are persons with rights that must be respected. Were they treated justly?
>
> What would Christian love and a just work-community require?

Since moral rules derive from principles, the questions we ask about rules and facts in a case are simply applications of the more general questions posed by overall principles. After all, what *does* the Lord require but that we love mercy, do justice, and walk humbly with God?

(4) But particular moral rules are not often directly deduced from principles alone. A fourth kind of input into ethical analysis is needed, background *control beliefs* about various areas of life and kinds of human activity. In the Manville case, control beliefs about the values intended for work and the workplace,

---

3. See, for example, C. J. H. Wright, *An Eye for an Eye* (InterVarsity Press, 1983), chap. 6; A. F. Holmes, "Biblical Justice and Modern Moral Philosophy," *Faith and Philosophy* 3 (1986): 429.

about employee rights, and about truth telling come into play. The abortion debate invokes beliefs about the sanctity of life and the right to privacy, about when personhood begins, and about sexual responsibility. A presidential candidate who plagiarized from other politicians' speeches was rejected in the primaries. Judgments about plagiarism rest on underlying beliefs about truth telling and property rights. Ethical issues regarding war and peacemaking require consideration of the purposes of government and the moral limitations to governmental uses of force. All these background beliefs about various areas of moral responsibility help shape moral rules.

This is where biblical thinking makes what is perhaps its most strategic contributions to ethics: in providing a biblical view of work and the workplace, or of punishment, of truth telling, of sex, and so on. To ask about the meaning and purpose of work is to ask about its values. In contrast to the Greek aristocratic view of work symbolized in the fact that the God of Aristotle neither created nor worked at all in the world, the biblical picture of God the creator incarnate as a carpenter of Nazareth gives dignity to the human worker and his stewardly tasks. In contrast to the acquisitiveness of the marketplace in today's individualistic society, the Bible pictures work as a divine calling, a stewardship in worshipful response to the Creator who gives liberally to all. In contrast to the Romanticist notion of work as a way to fulfill one's creative potential and gain self-satisfaction, the Bible says plainly that work requires wisdom and discipline, that it can build character, that it is a way of serving other people.

Distinctively Christian concepts of this sort derive from Scripture, but they are also informed by the history of Christian ethics. What the early church fathers said about the use of force, or the Reformers about work as vocation, can be very illuminating, especially when it is kept in the larger context of their theology. Christian ethics today should build on the insight of the church throughout its history and so avoid the provincialism and prejudice of late twentieth-century political, economic, and social outlooks. In any case, why reinvent the wheel when we can learn so much from what the Christian community has done before, particularly on Christian control beliefs about the values we should be pursuing in each area of life's responsibilities? The formation of conscience discussed in the previous chapter thus feeds into ethical analysis and decision making.

A further word is still needed about how ethical analysis works where conflicting obligations are present. The Manville managers might well have experienced a conflict between maintaining efficient and profitable production for the benefit of everybody connected with the company, and suspending production while upgrading the plant and retraining workers. Such dilemmas arise whenever moral obligations conflict or when no really good way exists of resolving a problem. What then can be done?

Two procedures are frequently employed. First, it is possible to rank the obligations involved in order of importance, giving preference to the most important. The ranking is based on those overall principles from which more specific rules and obligations arise. Suppose that in Amsterdam in 1943 you are hiding a Jewish friend in your attic when Gestapo agents demand to know where she can be found. Do you lie or do you tell the truth? Is truth telling more important than the preservation of innocent human life, especially when the truth would aid an unjust government in unjust violence against innocent life? To put it that way is to rank the conflicting obligations in relation to justice and compassion, or to respect for persons as ends in themselves. Control beliefs also are involved about the proper purpose of government and the moral limitation to its use of force. If those beliefs are correct, and the principles of justice and love are correctly applied, then God's will in the matter has been decided.

A second procedure is to develop moral rules (also based on overall principles) to govern exceptions to moral rules. In the case of the Gestapo and your Jewish friend, there are prima facie moral rules respecting the rights and liberties of citizens. Yet punishment of lawbreakers is also a moral responsibility, so rules are developed to limit punishment as an exception to the rules about rights and liberties: just cause must be shown, punishment must not be disproportionate to the crime, and innocent parties should be immune from arrest. Abuse of the power to punish is thereby avoided. But the arrest and deportation of Jews simply because they are Jews terribly misuses the powers of government and the power to punish. Is it not then morally justifiable to protect your friend? Would it not be a legitimate case for conscientious disobedience?

Penal codes are but one example of rules to govern exceptions to moral rules, so as to prevent abuses. Moral rules have also been developed for cases of conscientious and civil disobedience, and in medical ethics where the withdrawal of life-support systems is hedged by regulations intended to prevent arbitrary and immoral decisions; and "just war rules" spell out when and how there may be justifiable exceptions to the prima facie rule against using military force.

Ethical analysis, I have suggested, organizes our thinking, feeding in four kinds of input about a case; it weighs conflicting obligations in terms of a ranking of rules, and protects the process against abuse by means of rules based on overall moral principles.

DECISION MAKING

Although we have now identified the kinds of input required in a particular case, the decision does not automatically follow. Nor is it always easy when conflicting responsibilities leave one with moral ambiguity. But a decision-making model can nonetheless be suggested.[4]

---

4. See also Lewis B. Smedes, *Choices* (Harper and Row, 1986), and David E. Cook, *The Moral Maze* (SPCK, 1983) for discussion of moral decision making in Christian perspective.

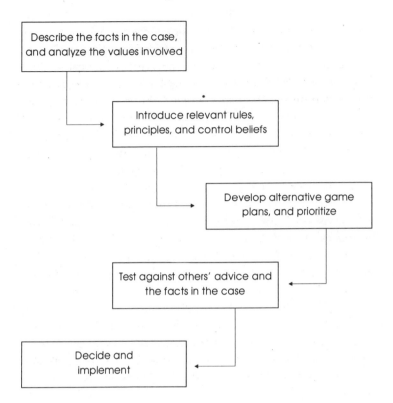

Notice that the various inputs we have discussed occupy only the first two steps. Their initial output requires further imagination in conceiving alternative possible game plans, which then need to be examined and ranked in order of moral preference. When questions of justice and love are involved, or respect for persons, that ranking can not be based simply on a cost-benefit analysis, nor even on an empathetic understanding of how people are likely to be affected, important a factor as that is. Principled moral decisions require a formed conscience with value-sensitivities which should have been developed long before the case in question arose; and responsible decisions require a high degree of care and personal disinterestedness—in a word, moral character.

In formulating and weighing alternative paths of action, however, it is always helpful to consider analogous cases (in history, fiction, ethics journals, etc.), where the ethical implications of alternative decisions have been developed. A vast body of such literature is available, and familiarity with at least some of it is invaluable.

Another helpful resource is acquaintance with role models in the business or profession, people whose principles, decisions, and policies make them exemplary. We should read about them, hear them speak, interact with them to gain the "feel" of their approach to things. Parents and teachers play this role for many young people, but the roster needs enlarging. They cannot be slavishly imitated, for each situation has its peculiar variables, yet it frequently helps to ask which option such a person might follow were he faced with this decision. The apostle Paul offered his own example in this fashion. The question "What would Jesus do?" is not irrelevant piety; it appeals to a perfect exemplar who has appointed us as his representatives in today's world. Taking this question seriously reaffirms Christian ethical principles and background beliefs and reinforces a Christian conscience. It can sharpen one's moral perception.

Decision making requires wisdom, a virtue far more elusive than the inputs and resources we accumulate, and far more basic than reasoning skills and decision-making models. Wisdom is the ability to see from a moral point of view *all* of the factors that should be considered, to recognize their due weight and understand their interrelatedness, to find the best way through a maze by seeing the problem as a whole and every part of it in the entire context. It affords the moral perception we need to choose between alternative plans for action. The need for wisdom keeps one from too quickly trusting her own judgment, and so introduces an intermediate step between the prioritizing of options and the final decision: test your judgment against the advice of others, go back and review with them the facts in the case. There is wisdom in the counsel of those whose experience and principles we respect, wisdom in having checks and balances on one's own thinking, wisdom in exposing our analysis to criticism by those more detached from the immediate problem or who might bring to it a larger or more objective viewpoint. It is important to run one's thinking about the options past the facts in the case again, testing the hypothetical against the actual, to ensure that all the facts and foreseeable consequences have been considered. A hospital may therefore have an ethics board, with an ethicist and representative clergy as well as experienced medical personnel. Some business corporations follow the same model, and some religious groups encourage their members to consult the community of faith in this way. New faculty members straight out of graduate school often benefit from the mentoring of senior professors. In any case, one who does not seek advice will certainly get an earful later; and one who does not test a proposal is asking for disaster.

So the decision emerges, cautiously and often slowly, and implementation follows. Even then a self-corrective process may continue, with opportunity to fine-tune a policy in the light of further experience, or even to reverse a decision and move to another option. There is little virtue in being stubborn.

TEACHING DECISION MAKING

What does all this say to questions about moral education? To start with curriculum, we do well to take stock of the particular competencies of the various disciplines and to ask where their contributions might best be introduced.

Start with the natural and social sciences, where many of the difficult cases that call for decisions arise. Plainly, their strength lies in understanding the facts in the case, in coming up with alternative game plans, and in anticipating both long and short-range consequences of various options that might be adopted. Scientists are in touch with written and unwritten rules governing the practices in their fields, existing codes of ethics, professional standards, and government regulations. Understanding as they do the practitioners and the values that often motivate them, natural and social scientists readily contribute not only on factual matters but also in analyzing the values and expectations involved.

What about biblical and theological studies? From what has already been said, we need their input on principles, moral rules, and control beliefs in providing moral exemplars (particularly the example of Jesus Christ), and in the rich resources of the history of Christian ethics. Philosophy meanwhile contributes analytic skills and conceptual clarification, experience in evaluating arguments and structuring the thinking process. It contributes well-honed theories about ethics, its bases and principles and forms of thought, and more recently a vast literature has arisen dealing with specific issues and particular case studies in virtually every area of applied ethics.

Meanwhile, history and literature and the arts interpret the human condition in both its outward manifestations and its inner reality, providing not just illustrations of moral problems, agents, and decisions, but insight into the ambiguities, tensions, and complexities of the moral life and a realism about moral ambiguity. They can nurture the moral imagination, elicit empathy, and provide the wisdom to see things whole.

The whole range of disciplines, then, potentially contributes to teaching moral decision making. While curriculum planning must decide when and how various disciplines can best make their contributions in the overall educational process, a first step is to ensure that the various departments recognize what they can contribute and incorporate it into their objectives and procedures. That will require faculty development and consensus building about both the importance of ethics and its place in the arts and sciences. A start can well be made regarding the range of objectives we have proposed by encouraging every department to identify which of these objectives readily falls within its competence, and what it can contribute thereto that will enhance ethical thinking and decisions.

Curricular possibilities will then emerge naturally: course components, ethics-intensive courses, resource people from other departments, team-taught courses, and so forth. For business or pre-med majors to graduate from a Christian college with no systematic exposure to business ethics or medical ethics and no experience in ethical decision making is educationally irresponsible. Somewhere in the curriculum, attention must also be given to ethical theories, to biblical ethics, and to requiring the student to think about control beliefs related to her particular field of endeavor. Plainly, departments of religion and of philosophy must make the teaching of ethics one of their major concerns.

Pedagogy should keep in mind the maturity level of students. Freshmen not yet used to thinking theoretically will find it difficult to take and stick to a moral point of view and work from overall principles. Kohlberg's developmental stages should be kept in mind in dealing with these cognitive processes. Freshmen may well be unable initially to think effectively beyond stages 3 or 4. It means teaching analytic thinking, and introducing sufficient cognitive dissonance to push a student further, although that needs to be done tolerantly and supportively. It means that active rather than passive learning is mandatory if students are to develop imagination or think their way through the complexities of a case toward a decision based on the kinds of input required. It may mean settling for a stage 4 or stage 5 conclusion to a class discussion. Gaining true wisdom will take years of experience beyond what four short nine-month spells in college can elicit, but we can at least help develop some of the cognitive skills and other elements on which wisdom will draw.

Various teaching suggestions have already surfaced:

Emphasize analytic thinking, rather than just the assimilation of theories and positions.

Focus on issues of human significance with which the student can readily identify.

Focus on problems that have no easy solutions.

Focus on viewpoints counter to student viewpoints to force critical thinking about what they and others think.

Offer exemplars or models.

Relate moral beliefs to the logical bases and underlying worldviews.

Avoid indoctrination, but also avoid the "cafeteria" approach.

Stir the imagination with "real life" scenarios and an array of possible outcomes to a moral dilemma.

Cultivate the ability to live with lack of conclusiveness, to tolerate moral ambiguity, to see that "good Christians" might legitimately disagree.

Remember that ethical decision making requires affective as well as cognitive involvement.

Teaching methods that require active learning are essential, whether it be a Socratic approach, or student debates, or position papers carefully responded to, or an ethics journal. The case-study method is widely favored, since it tends to preenact the kind of decision-making process one will often go through after college. The instructor assigns a case or two for discussion, acts as a member of the group so as to provoke careful analysis and argument, and guides the discussion through the necessary kinds of input to points of major importance. The aim is to arouse moral imagination, to give experience in ethical analysis, and to reach a final decision without foreclosing along the way. The student should learn how to secure the needed inputs, how to separate what is important from what is irrelevant, how to relate ethical theory to moral practice, and so how to make good ethical judgments. This will doubtless be of more value in some disciplines than others— namely, in those where moral issues are part of the daily decision-making process, as in health professions and business.

All of these methods, however, require more than simply discussion can provide. Some lecturing is usually necessary in introducing ethical principles and forms of moral reasoning and in setting an issue in context: a scientific or social context, and the context of what Christian ethics has said historically in that area. Of course students could research some of this independently, and in any case they need to learn how to do so—they will not always have instructors to do some of their homework for them!

That is why moral indoctrination is so inappropriate. Simply telling people what to decide will not teach them how to think through a new issue in the future and reach a wise decision for themselves. On the other hand, moral neutrality on the part of the teacher will not be helpful either: it implies there is little of major importance to choose between and, still more important, it denies the value of modelling moral concern and commitment. Some kind of moral advocacy is needed that will go beyond a neutral stance or Perry's kind of relativism, without engaging in unanalytic indoctrination. Discussion can, if necessary, be used to draw out the ethical dimension of a situation and identify the choices available. The student must then work at assessing the options. Perhaps the teacher's opinion is most appropriate at that juncture in the decision-making model where a proposal is tested against others' advice and the facts in the case. At that point, when the difficulties in deciding are to the fore, the teacher can readily raise questions about what is proposed, draw attention to facts or control beliefs or arguments that may be overlooked, and then advocate a counterproposal which seems in that light to be morally preferable. That kind of care and commitment in taking the moral point of view and pressing the analysis further, along with verbalized emphases that convey genuine moral feeling, will both commend the teacher's conclusion and model for the class what being a responsible moral agent is like.

Chapter Five

Developing Character

The biblical concept of righteousness extends significantly beyond forming the conscience and learning to make wise decisions. Righteousness is not just a matter of right conduct but a matter of the heart, not just a question of what I value and what I do, but of the kind of person I am at the core of my being. Scripture has various ways of speaking about this. Jesus blessed the "pure in heart" (Matt. 5:8), unalloyed, predictable, the same all the way through. James echoes this when he warns the "double-minded man" of his "unstable" ways (James 1:8). Paul offers his own example in persistently pressing toward the goal, regardless of the cost (Phil. 3:4-17), after reminding readers that Christ, our moral ideal, "took the form of a servant . . . and became obedient unto death" (Phil. 2:5-8). Solid, unwavering character is emphasized in all of this.

The root meaning of the word "character" refers to something cut or engraved into an object, that marks it unmistakably for what it is. So it is with moral character: it persists day after day whatever happens. It is not just a collection of occasional behaviors or of good intentions that never get implemented, but it is what I am solidly through and through, a matter of the heart. Someone who is weak-kneed and can't stand on his own feet morally, we call weak. Someone who outwardly behaves well but inwardly is jealous, hateful, selfish, or proud, we call a hypocrite. Someone who is inwardly well-intentioned but outwardly fails to follow through, we call irresponsible. But someone who is "true blue," solid all the way through, all the time, inwardly and outwardly alike, we say has moral character, a moral identity of his own. But character does not just grow like Topsy; it must be carefully, painstakingly cultivated. This is what our phase three is about.

Post-Enlightenment ethics so emphasized reasoning and decision making as to fragment morality into an array of particular acts. Correspondingly, sin has been atomized in the popular mind into a collection of particular thoughts and deeds: the typical college student thinks of sin and righteousness as specific behaviors flagged by do's and don'ts, rather than as a pervasive condition of the heart, a question of moral identity.

The ethics of virtue has recently received fresh attention. While it moves markedly beyond Enlightenment emphases on reasoned judgments, it still tends to focus on separate virtues considered individually, rather than on their interrelatedness in the moral identity of a person. For virtues and vices cluster together in an interwoven pattern that constitutes a person's character and defines who she is. As a person is in her heart, so she is; from the heart, said Jesus, proceed thoughts and deeds, and from its abundance the mouth speaks. Moral education needs to address these habits of the heart, not just reasoning processes or proper behaviors, but the shaping of the heart into Christlike moral identity.

There is a danger in any emphasis on the inner life, as a Quaker friend recently pointed out, the danger of a privatized morality that neglects social concerns. Examples abound of business people and politicians who have cultivated private virtues but neglected public justice. Inwardly they seem godly, but outwardly they remain secularized. Of course, the opposite danger is apparent too, of a legalistic conformity to the behavioral expectations of the Christian community without the corresponding inner dispositions. It is the danger of hypocrisy.

A Christian ethic should of course stand against both dangers, both privatism and hypocrisy, for truly virtuous character disposes one to act in certain ways, and genuinely Christian character will seek justice and love mercy as concomitants of walking humbly with God.

Virtue ethics and the ethics of action are not mutually exclusive. Recall James Rest's emphasis on the necessity of moral choice that puts moral values ahead of personal interests. That takes character. But in addition to disposing one towards right actions, virtue can provide moral guidance when we ask what is the fair or loving thing to do, or what a truly honest man would want to do in a given situation. A virtuous person will sometimes be sensitive to moral dimensions of a complex decision that one of lesser character would tend not to notice, or even brush aside. Virtue can enrich moral understanding and lead to better moral decisions.[1]

A few years ago I focussed some of my vacation reading on three books depicting the challenge of a new era: a biography of John Winthrop of the Massachusetts colony, a biography of Governor Bradford of the Plymouth plantation, and the book of Deuteronomy. All three shared the same driving concern for a just and compassionate society made possible by the law and grace of God. And all three emphasized the need for "wisdom," a virtue whose sensitivity to the overall picture and whose perception of the human dimension of things can contribute to far-reaching and good decisions. Similarly, virtues like compassion or courage enable one to see possibilities for the future that others might overlook. By sharpening moral perception, virtue can enhance moral decisions.

Both emphases are needed, both decision making and an

---

1. I am indebted here to an unpublished paper by Malcolm Reid, "A Sketch of a Christian Ethic of Virtues, Character Development and Moral Decision Making." See also Oliver O'Donovan, *Resurrection and Moral Order* (Eerdmans, 1986), chap. 10. Paul Nelson, *Narrative and Morality: A Theological Inquiry* (Penn. State Univ. Press, 1987), resists Hauerwas' tendency to stress the independence and sufficiency of virtue ethics.

ethic of virtues, and this extends responsibility for moral education to the entirety of campus life. Forms of moral reasoning and processes of decision making can be taught in the classroom, but the character of a student is influenced by experiences of every sort, more by personal relationships and the communities of which she is part than by classroom instruction. In considering the development of character, then, we shall have to broaden our horizons.

RESPONSIBLE AGENTS

We start where phases one and two left off. Phase one concerns sensitizing the conscience to right values—good ends we should desire and pursue and which therefore inform responsible behavior and action. Phase two requires the imagination to take the moral point of view and to approach decisions on a principled basis. When principled decisions, responsibly thought through and acted upon, become a matter of habit, something is happening inwardly. The person is developing character, becoming a responsible agent.

There is plainly a connection between character and conduct. "Character" refers to the kind of person one is, the agent who acts rather than just the actions. Actions and behavior patterns may well be indications of character, but not always so. They may be "put on" hypocritically, like socially approved masks to hide unacceptable motives and feelings, or they may be conformities socialized into us without inner conviction. A *responsible* agent, however, is one who makes a habit of acting reflectively, deliberately, and freely, and who *means* what she says and does. The inner reality corresponds to the outward appearance. There is oneness, integrity.

Earlier this century moral education went through a behavioristic stage that defined morality in terms of socially acceptable behaviors which it therefore sought to reinforce. Behavioral rules in the Christian college still sometimes seem more oriented in this direction than to character development, particularly when the emphasis that comes across is paternalistic and protective, or when it highlights penalties rather than personal responsibility. Yet the fact remains that habitual behaviors do nurture moral dispositions, and dispositions are what virtue is about.

Aristotle is the classic point of reference in this regard.[2] The moral training of children, he pointed out, requires the inculcation of habits, and habit formation in early years is the responsibility of parents and teachers. Authority and discipline are the pedagogs. But as children grow older the method must change. Adolescents, we know, tend to resist suggestions, and in their developing independence they repeatedly test the limits of authority. Something of the adolescent persists in all of us, Paul suggests, in that sinful passions are "aroused by the law" and so find occasion to work all kinds of covetousness (Rom. 7:5-8). Moral authority is important: the Westminster Catechism appropriately speaks of a threefold function of God's moral law in convicting us of sin, driving us to Christ, and providing a rule of life. But the moral authority even of God's law, as every Christian should know well, can only command: it cannot compel obedience, let alone produce character. Behavioral rules likewise will never ensure either conformity or character.

Aristotle's point was that behavioral habits must be developed *by choice* if they are to influence moral dispositions, choices that are repeated until they become habitual, until one is no longer inclined otherwise. In that sense a responsible agent is one in whom a habit of the heart is taking root and virtue is developing. This is no easy process, for it takes self-discipline and emotional self-control, and some people are more beset than others with a weakness of will that sabotages such moral growth.

What does this kind of moral growth entail? An education that helps form the conscience and develop good decision-

2. *Nicomachean Ethics* II.1–III.5.

making skills lays a needed foundation. The self-understanding afforded by values clarification raises awareness of the growth we need. Habits of principled moral thinking may readily be extended to self-examination. Then we are ready to set goals for ourselves, realistic goals for personal growth, and to cultivate habits and relationships conducive to achieving those goals. This is accepting responsibility for oneself.

It is easy to mouth high ideals while behaving in thought-less ways. The unthinking prankster "didn't mean to" do the harm his antics caused, and some people "let off steam" in highly inappropriate ways. This is being irresponsible. To ac-cept responsibility for oneself is to be accountable not only for what I intend, but also for what I do and say and what I am like towards others. It means acting reflectively and deliberately, not haphazardly or compulsively or under peer pressure. Accept-ing responsibility for oneself must become habitual in every area of life—from conscientious completion of course assignments to working at relationships and how we play.

Being responsible also means taking on responsibility for others rather than living for oneself alone. This is one contribu-tion that campus organizations and student service projects can make to character development. Assuming a good start has been made by consciousness-raising and sensitizing, respon-sible action is still needed, deliberate habits of acting in purpose-ful and measured ways in behalf of others. Student groups generally have no shortage of ideas for service projects: what they need is a fuller understanding of issues and social contexts plus guidance in selecting, planning, implementing, and eval-uating projects. Responsible action is not a matter of just doing something, doing it anyhow, but of choosing responsibly, plan-ning responsibly, preparing responsibly, and carrying through on it responsibly, and then learning how to do it better. This means accountability and calls for evaluation processes. But then tutoring inner-city children, an environmental cleanup project, voter registration, pressing for subsidized housing for the poor, social involvements of many sorts that make worthwhile contributions, can also provide ways for inculcating responsibility.

Responsibility is socially important, of value for what it can contribute to others, but it is important too for the kind of character it helps develop in the agent as a human being. It is deliberate habits of responsible action that, as Aristotle told us long ago, develop those dispositions of the heart he called virtues.

VIRTUES

The virtues that comprise character, like the "fruit of the Spirit" spoken of in Galatians 5, have to be cultivated with care. A virtue, as a settled moral disposition, involves desire, an inclination towards ends we ought to pursue: it thus has a strong emotional ingredient. Jonathan Edwards spoke of such desires as "affections" and wrote extensively on the nature and influence of religious affections. More recent writers like Stanley Hauerwas, recognizing that in current usage "desire" is oriented to pleasure, prefer "intention" so as to stress action-oriented choice. Yet they all agree in emphasizing the emotive dimension. Virtuous habits have a rational dimension in the deliberate choice of means to intended ends. But rational deliberation by itself is not the moving force; it is desire, operating with careful thought, that results in the repeated choices and actions that reinforce moral dispositions.

We can now see the relationship between values and virtues. In chapter three we defined values as good ends we ought to pursue. Right values are ideals of an objective sort, good ends whether we recognize them or not. Virtue is the habit of a heart firmly inclined toward right values, hungry and thirsty for them. The question, then, arises as to what can be done to further the development of virtue, how good habit-forming choices may be encouraged, how the right desires can become second nature. How do we train the heart?

It plainly goes beyond questions of curriculum and pedagogy to the entirety of college life, on campus and off. I say
"beyond" since, if values and virtues are as closely related as I
suggest, teachers would err as badly in shedding responsibility
for student character as they would in ignoring values. Values
are ends; virtues, in many cases at least, are positive dispositions
towards good ends. In influencing values we influence virtues.
And a teacher can encourage right dispositions by making
habitual tasks purposeful and satisfying, by encouraging informed, action-oriented decisions, and by modelling such
virtue-related things herself.

We should not ignore the help a classroom course on the
ethics of virtue could afford by getting students reflecting on a
particular virtue, how it manifests itself in attitude and action,
the emotions with which it is associated, and the psychology
involved. Self-understanding ensues, ideals and experiences
that might have been ignored now become desirable, personal
goals emerge, and the deliberate development of habits is
shown to be essential. This could make an immense difference
in the direction a person's moral development takes.

Whether in such a course, in counselling, or wherever,
goal-setting is an obvious, if neglected, way of coming at the
task. What particular virtue do I need to cultivate? Patience?
Self-discipline? In what attitudes and actions would it be evident? In what situations would such attitudes and actions be
called for? Let me anticipate now, therefore, how I shall behave
in those situations, inwardly and outwardly, and what I will do
to build the right habits.

But the onus for cultivating virtue, like transmitting
values, extends beyond the individual and the classroom to the
entire college community, and still beyond. Stanley Hauerwas
has written at length on the role the community and its story
play.[3] By finding my place in that story, I make it my story and
the community my community. Its story continues to unfold in

3. *A Community of Character* (Univ. of Notre Dame Press, 1981).

my story day by day, in the choices I make, the ends I desire, the habits I form. Because the story is about ends and means, about choices and habits, making it my story too means I make its ends mine, and its desires become my desires too.

Members of particular communities have their own particular stories. Old Testament Israel continually rehearsed what God had done, and their festivals celebrated that story. Scottish Covenanters and Anabaptist groups had their own stories too, and a particular kind of character still develops in these communities. The examples could be multiplied.

The Christian community has its own story, the gospel story and the whole history of God's redemptive activity in this world. It is a story about God and the kingdom of righteousness he says I should seek first and foremost. Choosing to seek it first and foremost must become a habit in all the choices I make about every kind of thing.

But consider also the ceremonies and rites of passage a community celebrates. Initiations can be critical: genuine repentance and conversion represent a turnaround of heart and mind from one way of life to another with changed intentions and new desires. Public baptism of adult converts symbolizes the spiritual cleansing that initiates believers into the community of faith, and the communion service celebrates their new life in Christ. Marriage too has its initiation ceremony and anniversary celebrations. Naturalization proceedings highlight an oath-taking ceremony in which new citizens are charged with responsibilities and privileges. In all these examples, initiation and celebration involve vows of loyalty made and renewed by members of a community. Colleges might do well to mark the induction of new students at the beginning of each academic year with similar ceremony, joining together in commitment to common ends they now ought to pursue with habits of thoughtful choice.

But initiation is not enough. The good intentions of today too easily become the embarrassment of tomorrow, and the new convert drifts away when too much stock is invested in the initiation and too little in habits of life together. Membership in community carries responsibilities which we must learn to practice by the disciplined development of heart and mind. Exemplars of Christian discipleship abound both historically and today in the Christian community; if we recognize the importance of exemplars, then we will want living exemplars within the college who incarnate both the virtues students need and the disciplined habits those virtues require.

In the community, friendships too are important: "fellowship" we call it within the church, referring to the comfortable togetherness which enriches our lives; but the Old Testament book of Proverbs relates friendship to moral development. Aristotle too regarded it as highly important, and he discussed various kinds of friendship at length. We probably give it much less adequate attention today. Consider that good friendship requires unselfishness, loyalty, sympathy, habitual consideration of another's needs; it contributes the wisdom and experience of others, common goals for moral development, emotional support in cultivating needed habits, the conscience of an alter ego as a prod to one's own. Prerequisite to friendship of this sort is having compatible values, good ends to be pursued together in habitual fashion. A friend's values are next in importance to my own.

Much of what I have said about how community bears on the development of virtue is rooted in Scripture—the story, remembering together what God has done and is doing among us, discipleship, exemplars, friends, and accumulated wisdom. While Scripture influences the moral life by pointing to all this, its influence is even more direct. Its imperatives and its theology, and most of all its faithful portrayal of the person and life of Christ, have a direct impact. The Scriptures themselves school our affections by penetrating, as the apostle says, into the thoughts and *intentions* of the heart, the seat of the virtues. It is the primary means God uses in nurturing the virtuous fruit of his Spirit.

Nor dare we ignore the hard reality of human depravity.

Aristotle realized that weakness of will inhibits wise choices, undermines the formation of good habits, and thereby badly affects character. The Christian recognizes an even more deadly depravity. Yet in the goodness of God people do develop virtues, including people devoid of Christian faith and experience; for a moral psychology continues to function in very significant measure in people everywhere. Aquinas suggested that natural processes make possible cardinal virtues like justice, prudence, courage, and temperance, which pertain to living with others in this world; yet virtues like faith and hope and love, which pertain to our life with God, depend on the grace of God. Whether or not a division can be made that clearly, we must recognize the operation of both the common grace of God in making virtue possible in people at large, and his special grace at work in believers. Every good thing comes from above.

The reality of human sinfulness is such that virtue is not always desired, self-discipline is not always achieved, bad habits are extremely hard to break. We may not even want to change. In a Christian context moral development must therefore go hand in hand with spiritual development—what theologians speak of as sanctification—and the means of grace by which the Holy Spirit frees people from sin's bondage and produces a hunger for righteousness that God can fill. But if in theory faith development and moral development have to go hand in hand, then in practice we must pursue them both. Spiritual life emphases that ignore the moral life, bypass the social responsibility of believers, fail to encourage responsible involvement in the life and work of the church, or otherwise assume a mistakenly individualistic approach will have limited effectiveness both ethically and spiritually. A privatized spirituality—one that concentrates on inner feeling and experiences, or divorces the religious from the "secular"—will be ineffectual; a more holistic spirituality is crucial, one that habitually practices the Lordship of Christ over every dimension of life, so that a hunger and thirst for righteousness, personal and social, becomes insatiable.

MORAL IDENTITY

In *The Closing of the American Mind,* Allan Bloom complains that students lack identity, a stable unifying core that ensures predictable moral behavior. For this problem, as for student relativism, he prescribes the great books of the liberal arts tradition as a common human heritage: they can impart a sense of identity in this day.

We take nothing from the importance of that liberal arts tradition by questioning whether it alone can restore identity to persons created to image God and to live in relationship to him. For the problem of personal identity is ultimately a psychological, moral, and spiritual one, not just one of *cultural* literacy and identity.

Arthur Chickering's *Education and Identity* set the problem before educators twenty years ago. A sense of identity, he maintained, has to do with the predictability of behavior consonant with one's purposes, the confidence that an inner sameness and continuity will be matched by a sameness and continuity for others. Where such identity exists, a sense of freedom characterizes interpersonal relations, and interests and purposes deepen. Identity means oneness, integrity, the integration of values into a consistent pattern, and the congruence of behavior with those values. In effect, then, identity gives inner strength. Personal identity is thus in large measure moral identity, and lack of moral identity will inhibit other aspects of personal growth as well as moral character itself.

Our concern is specifically with *moral* identity, however, and it is important also because without it values lack any ordered unity and overall virtue is wanting. A disorganized array of values can pull in every direction at once; and isolated virtues, if possible at all, remain incomplete alone, even distorted. The sadistic gangster may love his children but one would hardly say he is, as a person, loving. The unity of the virtues has been a concern of ethicists ever since Plato raised the question in his dialogs, for moral character is not a potpourri

69

of assorted dispositions but an integrated moral identity solid all the way through; character development is therefore the formation of a stable and predictable agent who can behave responsibly in all of life's relationships.

Two different philosophical traditions on personal identity are helpful in understanding the growth of moral identity. On the one hand empiricists and others from John Locke to the present day see personal identity grounded in experience and so dependent on the continuity of a person's memory. Some such accounts are quite individualistic, as if I find identity within the isolation of my own mind. On the other hand, phenomenologists from Hegel to Martin Buber, John Macmurray, and other recent thinkers stress the social nature of personal identity as it emerges out of relationships with others. I find myself in being a husband and father, a neighbor and teacher and friend.

Plainly, a Christian understanding of persons favors the more relational account, if we are created to live in relation to God and to do so in relation to other people and the physical world of which we are part. Yet the memory theory can point in that direction too, since memories are made up of relational experiences. Hauerwas' emphasis on "the story" is in effect an appeal to memory, and his emphasis on community and its story is an appeal to the memory of the community. The result is an account of personal identity that is well grounded theologically, philosophically, and psychologically too. And since relationships continue and memory in time grows longer, personal identity continues to develop and with it that moral identity which is the essence of character.

Reflection on moral identity and its importance is then naturally elicited by biography and by historical or literary characters, their virtues and vices, the kind of consistent identity they either exhibited or lacked, and the love that was their dominant characteristic. One of the major benefits of studying literature should be the understanding it affords of human beings and, mirrored thereby, a fuller and truer self-perception. By the same token, one benefit of the biblical literature is its realistic portrayal of biblical characters, complete with their virtues and vices. It acts like a mirror, the apostle says, in which we see ourselves as we are and go away resolved by God's grace to become what we have not yet been. If historical and literary characters direct attention to matters of moral identity we see the wisdom of that Christian piety that contemplates the person of Christ and his life on earth. As one fully human as well as fully divine Jesus is the perfect example: his moral identity was found in family and religious community in relation to the Father. And character like his is the goal.

But what kind of relationships unite the virtues into the integrated pattern which moral identity requires? Since virtues are dispositions towards good ends, the virtue that disposes one towards the highest, unifying end will order the rest. And since the highest end, the supreme good which gives all else its value, is God, it follows that love for God should unify the virtues. Both Augustine and Aquinas make love the integrating virtue, for we are ruled by what we love. Augustine argued that temperance is love keeping itself uncorrupted for God, and that justice is love serving God and therefore ruling all else well.[4] So too with other virtues: love for God gives Godward direction to them all. In that sense love is the highest and central virtue to be cultivated, and the Christian's moral identity takes shape in relation to God. Augustine's own *Confessions* elaborates this autobiographically in terms of the reforming and integrating of his own desires as a result of his conversion.

We come back therefore to the familiar theme that the highest good is a heart and life devoted to God. Teaching ethics as part of the integration of faith and learning requires the nurturing of faith and devotion. Moral education merges the modeling of an ethic with modeling love for God. Jesuit colleges, former president Frank Rhodes of Cornell University once noted, accordingly gave priority to the role of the

4. *On the Morals of the Catholic Church*, in *Basic Writings of St. Augustine*, vol. 1, ed. Whitney J. Oates (New York: Random House, 1948), pp. 319-360.

teacher in setting an example that would inspire students to a life of moral and intellectual excellence and spiritual commitment.[5]

In nurturing love for God, habits of heartfelt worship have to be central. The things a community says in song, recital, confession, reading, and preaching are all ways of talking about righteousness and moral character. It is the language of a community of moral discourse that makes its ultimate appeal to what God has done as the ground for human moral responsibility. Thereby it affirms who we are as a people, the people of God. It affirms an identity in terms of which we continue to form our consciences, shape our behavior, and solidify character.[6]

Character development, like spiritual growth and personal development more generally, is really a lifetime process. But college years are among the most formative, and an emerging moral identity helps set the direction that future development will take. Subsequent changes, of course, do occur, not only for the better but also sometimes for the worse. But college can establish goals and set a direction, and it can build bridges into the future by means of ongoing friendships that are established, institutional loyalties that persist, and the exemplars in various fields who continue to influence the graduates. Commencement, like landmark celebrations in other communities, should mark the beginning of a new stage in a lifelong process of developing character that grows increasingly responsible, increasingly virtuous, and that loves God with heart and mind and strength—a single-minded Christian moral identity that is, as we put it earlier, solid all the way through.

5. On the 200th Anniversary of Georgetown University, reported in *America*, August 5, 1959, pp. 54-60.
6. Paul Ramsey in *The Roots of Ethics*, ed. Daniel Callahan and H. T. Engelhardt, Jr. (Pilgrim Press, 1976), pp. 154-166.

Chapter Six

A Concluding Note: The Bible and Ethics

Reviewing the course that this discussion has taken, it becomes apparent that the Bible will play a major role in the kind of moral growth we envision. It is not as simple a role as Scripture is often given in popular presentations, for our objectives are more manifold, many of the issues more complex, and the biblical contribution itself far more varied than the layperson often imagines. Moral education is not a simple matter of asserting what the Bible says and backing it up by prooftexts: it involves the complexities and tangled situations in which we gain help from psychology, philosophy, and theology as well as the biblical text itself.

1. Prooftexting—that common practice of citing verses piecemeal and out of context in order to make a point—is inadequate. In the simple and straightforward case when someone asks if adultery is wrong, then a quick quotation from the Decalogue may be enough. But if the questioner wants to know "in this day and age" why God forbids adultery, or what other than his command makes it wrong, then the commandment itself is not enough. And if one asks precisely what constitutes adultery—for example, whether polygamous Old Testament

believers like Jacob were therein guilty of adultery—then too the prooftext by itself does not greatly help.

We need a more complete and unified picture than unrelated prooftexts can provide, an organized account of all the Bible has to say on the subject. This in turn must be kept in the larger setting of a biblical view of sex and marriage as a whole, and that in relation to the biblical doctrine of persons. To carefully consider the larger context of a text, then, we must look not only at its immediate setting in a particular chapter and book, and that chapter and book in their historical setting, but also at what is said on the topic in the gradually unfolding biblical revelation and at the overall theology in which it is grounded. Often, the still larger context of the accumulated wisdom of the ages and what human nature and human history teach us can illumine the biblical intent. That is why the history of Christian ethics is also important.

In effect, "context" includes (1) the immediate literary context; (2) the immediate historical context; (3) the overall picture in both the Old and New Testaments; (4) the overall theological picture of God, his nature and his purposes for creation, and of the nature of human persons; (5) the accumulated wisdom of the church on the ethical question being considered; and (6) the light general revelation may cast. At the same time the individual text must be carefully examined, although with a view to grasping the truth of the matter as a unified whole.

Consider, by way of example, the subject of capital punishment. Old Testament texts could be cited to allow capital punishment for ten different crimes, including adultery and cursing one's parents. Are we to conclude that this should be our practice today? Jesus rescued from her executioners a woman who had been arrested in the act of adultery (John 8). It seems evident that the Mosaic law was far more merciful than the almost arbitrary executions that were common in many other ancient lands, and Jesus presses even further the claims of mercy—also of justice—in his interchange with the woman's

74

would-be executioners. This larger picture therefore suggests that the Mosaic legislation might be viewed as the first step in a process of penal reform, which must always go on in a fallen world. Isolated proof texts are not enough.

2. Another mistake some people fall into is to assume that the Bible must have something specific to say about every ethical issue that may arise. This is plainly not the case. It certainly speaks to each of the broad "value areas" (like work, marriage, or the value of human life) that are common to all people of all cultures and times, and so provides invaluable control beliefs, but modern technology and modern society pose moral issues that the biblical writers could never have imagined, issues about genetic research, biological warfare, and nuclear wastes, for instance. Scripture is the final authority on matters of faith and conduct, to be sure, but it is not exhaustive. Its broad principles are always relevant, but other inputs from other sources, as we noted in previous chapters, also contribute.

The finality of Scripture does not make it the only source of moral understanding available. General revelation in ethical matters also is available. In the opening chapters of *Romans*, Paul plainly asserts that moral law is sufficiently accessible by natural means that everyone is held accountable; and the book of *Proverbs* is often regarded as traditional wisdom now passed on to us with God's authority. So if we do regard the Bible as our final moral authority, then we will also want to look at other ethical resources as well, of lesser worth though they be. We do well to listen to natural law arguments in ethics, and to assess what other ethical principles might contribute to Christian moral reasoning.

Granted that prooftexting is not a good use of Scripture and that the Bible is not exhaustive on ethical subjects, the fact remains that it touches every general area of human values, articulates overall moral principles that are binding in every area, and is loaded with instructive examples and applications from ancient cultures. Consider some varied forms its ethical teaching takes:

History and biography
Assertions about God's character
God's activity and purpose in the work of salvation
Theological perspectives on life's various involvements
The example of Christ
Stories and recorded incidents
Moral denunciations of human societies and behaviors
Proverbial moral wisdom
Qualities of godly character and life
Commandments and rules for living.

The list could go on. Lewis Smedes helpfully distinguishes four kinds of rules, not all of them moral rules.[1]

1. Absolute moral rules to which there are no exceptions, namely justice and love. In chapter four I called these "overall principles."
2. Rules with hardly any exceptions, for particular areas of responsibility.
3. Rules of strategy that may change with circumstances, like Paul's advice against eating foods offered to idols.
4. Rules of propriety that have cultural rather than moral significance and so are culturally variable, such as whether women should cover their heads.

3. When all the biblical input is considered, we readily recognize that it bears on the entire course we have followed in discussing moral education. It helps define objectives, and it speaks to all three phases: forming the conscience, making wise decisions, and developing moral character.

In regards to *forming the conscience,* the Bible's realistic account of people's lives and historical events makes one aware of a wide range of problems and helps sensitize the reader to the values involved. When Old Testament prophets expose the evils of their contemporaries, they are in effect engaged in

1. Lewis B. Smedes, *Choices* (Harper and Row, 1986), chap. 4.

values analysis and values criticism; so too in the Sermon on the Mount (the love of mammon, for example, or the man who built his house on the sand), and some of Paul's epistles (e.g., his censure of some Corinthian Christians). The wisdom literature of the Old Testament is about values through and through, the books of Proverbs and Ecclesiastes most of all. This is the stuff that has shaped the Christian conscience for centuries.

When we think of what *decision making* requires, the biblical contribution again is immense. To step outside our own interests and take the moral point of view, we said, takes imagination. That is precisely what the Bible helps us do. It steps outside the immediate scene and speaks from another standpoint: "Thus says the Lord," cried the prophet. The moral point of view is far more accessible to those who have soaked up the language and standpoint of the Bible. And like any good literature it fuels the imagination with its realism about people and their choices, and the consequences in it all.

Moral reasoning is an obvious area for biblical input. The biblical concern for justice and love provides overarching principles; the moral law gives rules, case studies abound, and the background beliefs that direct us to the ends we should desire are also shaped by Scripture. Meantime, exemplars abound of responsible agents, and the virtues and vices are highlighted continually: character development is the Bible's overall moral concern.

Much of this is about the content of Scripture and what it teaches. But it also shows the Bible as an enabler: it sensitizes the conscience, fires the imagination, inspires faith, hope, and love. It is a primary means of grace in the work of the Holy Spirit.

These last paragraphs catalog a range of biblical contributions. One that they omit, the context of all the others, is that the biblical literature is the story of our faith and community. Since the Bible is an historical account, its ethical materials are historical documents, themselves part of the Christian story, our story as Christians, our heritage, our community in relation to

God. And what community does in nurturing virtue and moral character, biblically oriented community does in the lives of believers, and more. More, of course, since it also points us to Christ, and because of the Spirit of God.

The role of Scripture in moral education is then both necessary and various, relevant to each objective we have proposed. Yet it still does not substitute for hard thinking—indeed it requires it. Nor can it bypass the processes of moral psychology, since it describes so accurately what goes on in the heart. To make good use of the Bible on ethics, then, we need to know its resources. My suggestion is that the reader explore them in relation to those of the eleven objectives in chapter 1 with which in particular she is concerned. The bibliography that follows identifies helpful materials on this and other topics that these chapters have introduced.

Bibliography

I. MORAL EDUCATION

Aristotle. *Nicomachean Ethics*.

Baum Robert J. *Ethics and Engineering Curricula*. Hastings-on-Hudson, N.Y.: Hastings Center, 1980.

Beck, C. M., B. S. Crittenden, and E. V. Sullivan, eds. *Moral Education*. Paramus, N.J.: Paulist-Newman Press, 1971.

Callahan, Daniel, and Sissela Bok. *Ethics Teaching in Higher Education*. New York: Plenum Press, 1980.

Chickering, Arthur. *Education and Identity*. San Francisco: Jossey-Bass, 1969.

Christians, Clifford G., and Catherine Covert. *Teaching Ethics in Journalism Education*. Hastings-on-Hudson, N.Y.: Hastings Center, 1980.

Clouser, K. Danner. *Teaching Bioethics: Strategies, Problems, and Resources*. Hastings-on-Hudson, N.Y.: Hastings Center, 1980.

Dykstra, Craig. *Vision and Character: A Christian Education Alternative to Kohlberg*. Mahweh, N.J.: Paulist Press, 1981.

Fleishman, Joel L., and Bruce L. Payne, *Ethical Dilemmas and the Education of Policymakers*. Hastings-on-Hudson, N.Y.: Hastings Center, 1980.

Hauerwas, Stanley. *Character and the Christian Life: A Study in Theological Ethics*. San Antonio, Tex.: Trinity University Press, 1975.

Heath, Douglas H. *Growing Up in College*. San Francisco: Jossey-Bass, 1968.

Joy, Donald M., ed. *Moral Development Foundations: Judeo-Christian Alternatives to Piaglet-Kohlberg*. Nashville: Abingdon Press, 1983.

Kelly, Michael J. *Legal Ethics and Legal Education*. Hastings-on-Hudson, N.Y.: Hastings Center, 1980.

Kohlberg, Lawrence. *The Philosophy of Moral Development*. New York: Harper and Row, 1981.

McGrath, Earl. "Careers, Values and General Education." *Liberal Education* 60 (Oct. 1974): 281-303.

Morrill, Richard. *Teaching Values in College*. San Francisco: Jossey-Bass, 1980.

Perry, William. *Forms of Intellectual and Ethical Development in the College Years*. New York: Holt, Rinehart and Winston, 1970.

Powers, Charles W. *Ethics in the Education of Business Managers*. Hastings-on-Hudson, N.Y.: Hastings Center, 1980.

Raths, Louis, Merrill Harmin, and Sidney Simon. *Values and Teaching*. Columbus, Ohio: C. E. Merrill Books, 1966.

Reamer, Frederic. *The Teaching of Social Work Ethics*. Hastings-on-Hudson, N.Y.: Hastings Center, 1982.

Rest, James. *Moral Development: Advances in Research and Theory*. New York: Praeger, 1986.

Rich, John Martin, and Joseph L. Devitis. *Theories of Moral Development*. Springfield, Ill.: C. C. Thomas, 1985.

Rosen, Bernard, and Arthur Caplan. *Ethics in the Undergraduate Curriculum*. Hastings-on-Hudson, N.Y.: Hastings Center, 1980.

Sherman, Lawrence. *Ethics in Criminal Justice Education*. Hastings-on-Hudson, N.Y.: Hastings Center, 1981.

Simon, Sidney, and H. Kirschenbaum, eds. *Readings in Values Clarification*. San Francisco: Winston Press, 1973.

Stiles, Lindley, and Bruce D. Johnson, eds. *Morality Examined: Guidelines for Teachers.* Princeton, N.J.: Princeton Book Co., 1975.

The Teaching of Ethics in Higher Education: A Report by the Hastings Center. Hastings-on-Hudson, N.Y.: Hastings Center, 1980.

Warwick, Donald P. *The Teaching of Ethics in the Social Sciences.* Hastings-on-Hudson, N.Y.: Hastings Center, 1980.

Wolterstorff, Nicholas, *Educating for Responsible Action.* Grand Rapids, Mich.: Eerdmans, 1980.

II. THE BIBLE AND ETHICS

Beach, Waldo, and H. Richard Niebuhr, eds. *Christian Ethics: Sources of the Living Tradition.* New York: Ronald Press, 1955.

Birch, Bruce C., and Larry L. Rasmussen. *Bible and Ethics in the Christian Life.* Minneapolis: Augsburg Publishing, 1976.

Cook, David E. *The Moral Maze: Way of Exploring Christian Ethics.* London: SPCK, 1983.

Curran, Charles E., and Richard A. McCormick. *The Use of Scripture in Moral Theology.* Mahwah, N.J.: Paulist Press, 1984.

Gustafson, James M. *Protestant and Roman Catholic Ethics: Prospects for Rapprochement.* Chicago: University of Chicago Press, 1978.

Hauerwas, Stanley. *The Peaceable Kingdom: A Primer in Christian Ethics.* Notre Dame: University of Notre Dame Press, 1983.

Higginson, Richard. *Dilemmas: A Christian Approach to Moral Decision Making.* London: Hodder and Stoughton, 1988.

Kaye, Bruce. *Using the Bible in Ethics.* New York: Grove Books, n.d.

Mott, Stephen C. *Biblical Ethics and Social Change.* New York: Oxford University Press, 1982.

_____. *Jesus and Social Ethics.* New York: Grove Books, 1984.

O'Donovan, Oliver. *Resurrection and Moral Order: An Outline for Evangelical Ethics*. Grand Rapids, Mich.: Eerdmans, 1986.

Ogletree, Thomas W. *The Use of the Bible in Christian Ethics: A Constructive Essay*. Philadelphia: Fortress Press, 1983.

Smedes, Lewis B. *Mere Morality: What God Expects from Ordinary People*. Grand Rapids, Mich.: Eerdmans, 1983.

_____. *Choices*. San Francisco: Harper and Row, 1986.

Spohn, William C. *What Are They Saying about Scripture and Ethics?* Mahwah, N.J.: Paulist Press, 1984.

Thielicke, Helmut. *Theological Ethics*. Philadelphia: Fortress Press, 1966.

Verhey, Allen. *The Great Reversal: Ethics and the New Testament*. Grand Rapids, Mich.: Eerdmans, 1984.

Wright, Christopher J. H. *An Eye for an Eye: The Place of Old Testament Ethics Today*. Downers Grove, Ill.: InterVarsity Press, 1983.

Wolterstorff, Nicholas. *Reason within the Bounds of Religion*. Grand Rapids, Mich.: Eerdmans, 1976.